A Practitioner's Tool for Child Protection
and the Assessment of Parents

A Practitioner's Tool For Child Protection and the Assessment of Parents

Jeff Fowler

Jessica Kingsley Publishers
London and Philadelphia

First published in the United Kingdom in 2003
by Jessica Kingsley Publishers
116 Pentonville Road
London N1 9JB, UK
and
400 Market Street, Suite 400
Philadelphia, PA 19106, USA
www.jkp.com

Library of Congress Cataloging in Publication Data
Fowler, Jeff, 1947-
    A practitioner's tool for child protection and the assessment of paretns / Jeff Fowler.
    p. cm.
    Includes bibliograhical references and index.
    ISBN 1-84310-050-9 (pbk. : alk. paper)
    1. Child abuse--United States--Prevention. 2. Abusive paretns--United States. 3. Child
abuse--Law and legislation--United States. 4. Family social work--United States. I. Title.
HV741 .F69 2002
362.76'5'0973--dc21   200203472

British Library Cataloguing in Publication Data
A CIP catalogue record for this book is available from the British Library

ISBN 978 1 84310 050 8

Printed and Bound in Great Britain by
Athenaeum Press, Gateshead, Tyne and Wear

CONTENTS

Acknowledgements 7

Introduction 9

Introduction to the practitioner's tool 14

Using the practitioner's tool 17

CHAPTER 1: STARTING ASSESSMENT 19

1.1 Beginning the assessment 20

1.2 The risk indicator checklist 21

1.3 The core assessment 31

1.4 The assessment plan 32

1.5 Introducing the case study 36

1.6 The assessment agreement 39

1.7 The assessment interviews 43

1.8 The first assessment session 47

1.9 Assessing the parents 48

CHAPTER 2: COLLECTING THE DATA FOR ASSESSMENT 49

2.1 The family structure 50

2.2 Chronology 51

2.3 Experiences from childhood 56

2.4 Education 66

2.5 Employment 69

2.6 Perception of self 70

2.7 Ideal self 81

2.8 Self-esteem 82

2.9 Exploring whether people
are organised or disorganised, rigid or flexible 85

2.10 Exploring dominant and submissive behaviour 88

2.11 Alcohol abuse 91

2.12 Drug abuse 94

2.13 Anger and violence 98

2.14 Schedule 1 offences 105

2.15 Criminal history 107

2.16 Health 110

2.17 Previous relationships 112

2.18 Present relationship 116

2.19 Parenting skills and abilities 127

2.20 Perception of children 129

2.21 Perception of being a parent 134

2.22 Parenting and stress 137

2.23 Parenting and the needs of children 142

2.24 The child 147

2.25 Attachment 149

2.26 Home environment 150

2.27 Finances 153

2.28 Child protection concerns 154

2.29 Evaluating the information 157

CHAPTER 3: ASSESSMENT: THE CASE STUDY 171

3.1 The case study assessment 172

3.2 Positive outcomes from assessment 189

3.3 Conclusion 192

A guide to the Children Act 1989 194

Some terms from child protection 199

Appendix: Exercises 203

References 248

Acknowledgements

To Alison Swales for her comments and suggestions.

To Judith Dodd for her comments, suggestions and meticulous attention to detail.

And most of all to Jacki Pritchard, who inspired me to begin the book and without whose support, encouragement and expertise it would never have been completed.

INTRODUCTION

I have worked as a residential and field social worker and manager for thirty-two years. Apart from a brief period at the beginning of the 1970s, all of that experience has been working with children and their families. I have been the principal of a large residential assessment centre, a fieldwork social worker and field social work manager. In addition I have been the advisor for children and families in a social services department, the social work advisor to a university, and had line management responsibility for children and family services, including fostering, adoption, child protection, court services and day care. I have also been a guardian ad litem panel manager.

In 1990 I left social work senior management to become a guardian ad litem and to develop an independent social work practice, which has included training, consultancy and assessment work in child protection. I presently act as the Independent Person to the Hesley group, which provides residential care for children and adults with learning disability and challenging behaviour. I am the Quality Standards Assessor for the National Association of Independent Resources for Children. I undertake children and family assessments in private and public law and am an expert witness to the High Court on issues involving adults with learning disability. I work as a member of the Children and Families Court Advisory and Support Service (CAFCASS), representing children in public law and specified proceedings.

I started practice as a social worker at the beginning of the 1970s. Like many others at the time, I was unqualified. I had energy, enthusiasm and commitment, but little theoretical skill and knowledge. I had no understanding of child protection, but gained some good experience of helping families who were struggling to manage either their children, themselves or both.

I was fortunate to qualify in social work sooner than most colleagues. I was introduced to the foundations of social work theory and practice and, although I was inspired to go out and 'change the world', I found I had learned nothing significant about child abuse.

Returning to practice in a deprived area in the Northeast of England, I was able to work positively in order to keep families together, and help families who were struggling to manage.

The work which I undertook with families where child protection was an issue usually involved neglect, and that was often identified using common sense rather than professional skills. Where physical injuries to children were encountered, the most severe ones diagnosed themselves, and sometimes others went unrecognised as child protection matters. Emotional neglect, sexual abuse and Munchausen syndrome by proxy were neither part of my vocabulary nor my knowledge base. I feel sure that like many others who reflect on their practice in those 'early days', I can only apologise to the children whom, through lack of knowledge and expertise, I failed to recognise as victims of abuse.

The informing legislation at the time was the Children and Young Persons Act 1969. The main constructs for orders to be made were that the child's proper development was being avoidably neglected or prevented, her/his health was being impaired, s/he was being ill-treated or exposed to moral danger, was beyond parental control, not attending school, or guilty of an offence (excluding homicide). The child also had to be in need of care or control.

The next piece of child care legislation, the Child Care Act 1980, did not affect the criteria for protecting children. It introduced a duty on local authorities to diminish the need to receive children into care or keep them in care. An era of 'preventative social work' was born and the focus of social work intervention changed. Local authorities developed services, for example Family Centres, to enable families to remain together in the community.

However, the 1980s produced a growing awareness of the extent of child abuse, and the need to have dedicated systems to accommodate and respond appropriately to this. Local authorities were required to establish inter-agency child protection committees, systems for child protection case conferences and child protection registers. These became the foundation for the development of a framework from which current child protection, in all its aspects, has evolved.

The 1980s also saw child protection catapulted into the spotlight by a series of inquiries:

- in 1985 'A Child in Trust' reporting on the death of Jasmine Beckford (London Borough of Brent 1985).

- in 1987 'Whose Child', reporting on the death of Tyra Henry (London Borough of Lambeth 1987)

- in 1987 'A Child in Mind', reporting on the death of Kimberley Carlile (London Borough of Greenwich 1987)

- in 1988 'Report of the Inquiry into Child Abuse in Cleveland 1987' was published (Cleveland Report 1988).

The impact of these on child protection services was profound. The management of child abuse and the concept of child protection as the responsibility of all professionals in the field of child care became part of policies and procedures.

Significantly, the Social Services Inspectorate had concluded from the inspection of local authorities that there was a need for a more structured and systematic approach to the assessment of cases where child abuse was suspected or alleged.

In 1988 the Department of Health published *Protecting Children. A Guide for Social Workers undertaking a Comprehensive Assessment* (DoH. 1988). For the first time practitioners had a model for the collection of information about families where there were child protection concerns. The 'Orange Book', as it became affectionately known, contained 167 questions which enabled information to be collected. It became the basis for comprehensive assessments for the next twelve years. Although it has had numerous critics over the years, it has also served professionals in the field of child protection extremely well and helped protect many children who have been abused or at risk of abuse.

On 14 October 1991, the Children Act 1989 was implemented. Historically, child care legislation has been updated every ten years or so to take account of changes in practice, accommodate lessons learned from inquiries and incorporate case law. The Children Act 1989 also took the opportunity to consolidate private law and public law proceedings into one piece of legislation.

Importantly, the Children Act 1989 introduced the concept of 'significant harm' and for the first time enabled 'risk of future significant harm' to be used as grounds for making orders. Predicting what might happen to children of a family in the future, based upon an evaluation of what has happened in that family in the past, brought renewed professional accreditation, and with that all of the attendant responsibility and accountability.

Working Together under the Children Act 1989 was published in 1991 by the Department of Health in conjunction with the Home Office and Department of Education. It addressed issues pertinent to the implementation of the Children Act 1989.

In December 1991 the United Kingdom ratified the United Nations Convention on the Rights of the Child. Article 19 requires that legislative, social and educational measures should be taken to protect children from any form of abuse whilst in the care of their parents and any other person, and appropriate systems should be in place to investigate and report on issues of child protection.

During the 1990s there have been further inquiries. Sadly, some of these focused on incidents of abuse whilst children were 'in care', for example 'pindown' in Staffordshire and Leicestershire. Others were commissioned because of the inappropriate intervention of child protection workers, for example the removal of children from their families in Orkney and Rochdale.

There were also innovations in practice. For example, in 1992 the *Memorandum of Good Practice* (*on video-recorded interviews with child witnesses for criminal proceedings* (HMSO 1992)) introduced the concept of the joint interview by social workers and police officers of children who were thought to have been abused.

In 1999 the Department of Health, Home Office and Department of Education published *Working Together to Safeguard Children*, a guide to inter-agency working to safeguard and promote the welfare of children. This document incorporated key findings from *Child Protection: Messages from Research* (DoH 1995) and responses made in *The Government's Response to the Children's Safeguards Review*. It required those in health, education, police, social services, probation, and others involved in child protection, to work together to promote children's welfare and protect them from abuse and neglect, and replaced *Working Together under the Children Act 1989*.

In 2000 the *Framework for the Assessment of Children in Need and their Families* was published by the Department of Health in conjunction with the Home Office and the Department for Education and Employment (DoH 2000). The framework was developed to provide a systematic way of collecting, recording and analysing information about children in need and their families. It is already being referred to as the 'Lilac Book'. It reflects the principles contained within the United Nations Convention on the Rights of the Child, and the Human Rights Act 1998.

The 1990s saw an enormous development in the knowledge base, understanding and expertise of child protection workers, as well as significant developments in the infrastructure which informs systems and services. The concept of an inter-agency, multi-disciplinary approach to child protection is now enshrined in policy, procedure and practice. Like many others I am sure, I have needed to work very hard to keep up to date with the ever expanding knowledge base in child protection and the implications for my practice. This increase in awareness, expertise, skills and knowledge has been both exciting and, at times, slightly frightening. A substantial theoretical base has been published to educate and inform. Despite the constant frustrations of limited resources, practitioners are now better equipped than ever before to deal with the complex issues which child protection and the assessment of families create. I hope that readers will find that the training material in this book provides further assistance to those working in this very demanding field. I hope that those professionals who provide training will find that this book increases the range of their materials and teaching information.

INTRODUCTION TO THE PRACTITIONER'S TOOL

This practitioner's tool recognises that children who have suffered significant harm or who are at risk of suffering significant harm are children in need. It does not seek to replace the *Framework for the Assessment of Children in Need and their Families* (DoH 2000) in any way, and is designed to provide additional material which can be used in conjunction with that framework, where workers are undertaking assessments in which child protection and the investigation of child abuse are significant issues.

It presumes that workers undertaking assessments are qualified and experienced to do so. It further presumes that workers are either experienced in the field of child protection or are being supervised/mentored by someone with such experience. The tool uses the experience of professionals who are working in this complex and demanding field and is currently being used to undertake the assessment of parents. In its presented form it has been designed to respond to the changing demands on time-scales, resources and the provision of services, as identified in the *Framework for the Assessment of Children in Need and their Families* (DoH 2000).

Assessments are inter-agency and multi-disciplinary. Workers should work individually and collectively to produce assessments which provide the best understanding of parents and issues of child protection. Whilst the social worker might be seen as the lead worker or key worker, other professionals have crucial contributions to make. Different fields of expertise and skill provide added knowledge for collection and evaluation of the information. In this way the assessment becomes a product of the combined skills of all of the workers. For example, health visitors have a unique knowledge and understanding of the developmental milestones which a child would be expected to reach, and their contribution in this area adds to the quality of the assessment produced. All professionals involved in the life of the child should be seen as members of the team which constructs the assessment of the parents. All should decide individually and collectively how their contribution fits into the whole.

The tool is child-centred and family-focused. Reports prepared using this tool are currently used in public law and specified proceedings, and are recognised as providing information on the basis of which critical decisions can be made about children and their families.

The tool incorporates the concepts and requirements of the *Framework for the Assessment of Children in Need and their Families*. It incorporates the three domains on which the new assessment framework is based.

Professionals undertaking child protection assessments using the tool will construct an understanding of parents using methods of collecting and evaluating information in a systematic way. This tool will be of value for practitioners new to assessment work because it provides easy-to-follow guidance through the complete assessment process and offers a case study that leads to an assessment report. Experienced practitioners will benefit from the consistent quality that results from using this tool.

Whilst recognising the importance of an assessment of the needs of children, and the specific connection between those needs and the abilities and skills of their parents, the tool concentrates specifically on the assessment of parents. Workers would therefore be expected to use this tool alongside the *Framework for the Assessment of Children in Need and their Families*.

The tool is supported by a case study which concentrates on one family, giving readers the opportunity to learn how the information is collected and evaluated. It therefore closely resembles practice.

The assessment process is supported by checklists which have been constructed from practice experience. Neither prescriptive nor exhaustive, they are designed to be used alongside the Family Pack of Questionnaires and Scales which forms part of the *Framework for the Assessment of Children in Need and their Families*, where appropriate, or as dedicated areas of assessment.

The checklists are designed to be easily reproduced for use in individual sessions within the assessment process. They are provided for within each of the key areas. Some of the checklists are for guidance only, indicating aspects which can be explored at the discretion of the worker. Some are only of value if they are used in their entirety, for example the 'checklist for self-esteem' (pp.83ff.). An indication is provided before each checklist as to the recommended use. There has been considerable debate over the years as to the value or otherwise of checklists, and no doubt their use will have supporters and critics both now and in the future. This tool uses checklists because they assist the consistent and systematic collection of information. There is, of course, an inbuilt degree of flexibility, in that workers can use them selectively within the unique context of each assessment. The checklists are not designed to be simply 'tick-box' documents. They are a tool for exploring the complex nature of people, relationships, concepts, skills and abilities.

It is important that workers do not use the checklists as 'stand-alone' sources of information. They should be used to confirm observations or opinions which have come from the entire assessment process. Workers should be alert to the possibility that, in order to reflect themselves in a different light, people may not be entirely truthful with the answers they give to checklist questions.

The tool is not designed to be rigid. More experienced practitioners may wish to incorporate their own material or exclude some of the checklists.

In identifying the needs of children and their families, the assessment information collected should be considered within the context of other information and existing reports, for example psychiatric reports. The greater the extent of professional information, the more likely it is that the decisions made will serve the best interests of the children and their families.

USING THE PRACTITIONER'S TOOL

The practitioner's tool is designed to accommodate the time-scales established by the *Framework for the Assessment of Children in Need and their Families* (DoH 2000).

- **within one working day** of a referral being received, or new information about a family being made available, there will be a decision about the appropriate response which is required.

- **within a maximum of seven working days** an **initial assessment** will be undertaken in respect of each child about whom there is concern. The parameters of the *Assessment Framework* should be addressed, although the extent of the assessment will be determined by the nature of the concerns. The initial assessment should enable decisions to be made which will safeguard and promote the welfare of the child. In particular, the extent to which the child is in need, the range and nature of services which are required, within what time-scale and how services will be provided should all be established. Child protection concerns must be addressed.

  The initial assessment may decide that a more detailed assessment, a core assessment, is needed to provide a fuller understanding of the needs of the child and family.

- **within a maximum of thirty-five working days** a **core assessment** will be undertaken. This assessment will be comprehensive: it will address all concerns and give an understanding as to whether or not the family is able to look after its children in ways which will safeguard and promote their welfare. It will identify what range of services are required to maintain children within their family, and to satisfy their physical, emotional and educational needs. It can also be used as a tool to make the important decisions about any child who cannot be safely looked after within the family.

The Department of Health has published an Initial Assessment Record and Core Assessment Record which are contained within the *Framework for the Assessment of Children in Need and their Families* (Assessment Recording Forms).

This tool contains a risk indicator checklist (pp. 23ff.) designed for use in identifying and collecting essential information, and which can be used alongside the initial assessment record.

The risk indicator checklist can also be used as a 'stand-alone' document. It is particularly useful where child protection decisions need to be made. Alternatively, the information contained within the risk indicator checklist can be used as part of the core assessment information. The completed risk indicator checklist enables an evaluation of current information. It also identifies those areas where insufficient knowledge exists and more information is needed. This will help to focus on how the initial or core assessment is planned.

The assessment component of this tool provides the reader with information, checklists and a process of evaluation to use in making the important decisions at the completion of the core assessment stage.

The risk indicator checklist can also be used as part of a child protection investigation. Such investigations are informed by the Children Act 1989, Section 47. This section identifies the responsibility which local authorities have to investigate the circumstances of any child in their area who they suspect is suffering, or likely to suffer, significant harm, and decide whether they should take any action to safeguard and promote the child's welfare. An analysis of the information contained within the checklist will help professionals to evaluate the level of harm which a child has suffered or is at risk of suffering. It will also provide a more complete picture of the strengths and weaknesses which exist within the family. In that way a decision about what response is required is likely to be more inform

CHAPTER 1

Starting Assessment

1.1 BEGINNING THE ASSESSMENT

Establishing what information is already available

In many cases there is already a considerable amount of information available from statutory sources, for example, social service departments, police, health, education. Additionally, the voluntary sector, for example, the NSPCC, Children's Society, Barnados, may have important information about families. An assessment is as much an evaluation of currently held information as it is the collection and evaluation of new information.

Where there has been significant previous involvement with child protection agencies, substantial file information is likely to exist. Where the family has not previously been known, there will be no information. Checks within the inter-agency, multi-disciplinary network of agencies can establish what is already known about the family. It is important that before any assessment work is undertaken, existing information should be collected and evaluated.

A search through the social services department file will usually identify other professionals who have been involved, and this might include:

- other social services departments
- voluntary organisations
- family centres
- health services
- probation
- schools
- police.

Access to the information held by others on their files will be helpful. In the absence of that, information is often on the social services department file. Case conference minutes will include reports and comments from other departments and agencies.

Wherever possible, contact with professionals currently involved is essential, and a key element in collecting up-to-date information. Helpful information usually held on professional files includes:

- child protection case conference minutes
- reviews
- core group minutes

- reports for court

- statements filed in previous proceedings

- centile charts (a medical record of the height, weight and head circumference of a child).

What is known about the source of the information

Information from professional sources would normally be given more weight than information from non-professional sources.

Information from professional sources with experience or expertise in child protection and child care should be weighted accordingly.

Information from within the family, neighbourhood, or other sources must be weighed against knowledge about relationships, difficulties and disputes. For example, an allegation made by a neighbour with whom the family is in dispute may be influenced by that dispute.

Anonymous information should not be dismissed out of hand, but without corroboration it should never be used as the primary source of an assessment area.

Where to begin

The risk indicator checklist is a tool which provides an overview of the family from a specific child protection focus. It records information that is already known about the family, and should always be completed as a first step in every instance of assessment. It enables the systematic listing of positive and negative indicators. From this, workers will be able to identify:

- the level of known risk about the family

- how that risk is currently being managed

- in what areas the family is felt to be functioning at an acceptable level

- the key areas in which insufficient information is available for making decisions.

1.2 THE RISK INDICATOR CHECKLIST

The first alert of a child protection issue is likely to come by way of a referral to the social services from another agency or outside source. Usual sources include the police, who may have been called to a domestic disturbance, a health visitor concerned about the welfare of a child following a home visit, or relatives, friends or neighbours. Schools are frequently a source of referral, as children find adults whom they trust and to whom they feel able to make disclosures. Teaching staff have contact with a child on an almost daily basis and are able to detect potential child protection signals, for example, changes in behaviour, response, emotional well-being.

The social service department is under a duty to investigate such child protection concerns (Children Act 1989, Section 47) and is likely to provide the lead workers where such investigations are necessary.

The risk indicator checklist is a tool to aid professional thinking and decision-making in the area of child protection. It is used to evaluate information currently known about individual families in order to identify the extent to which they are a family in need, and indicate whether or not intervention may be necessary in order to safeguard and promote the welfare of the children. The risk indicator checklist should be completed in consultation with all professionals who are involved with the family. It should not be used in isolation as a document of authority, nor as the only source of information on which child protection decisions are made. However, it is a significant tool in the child protection process. It is a guide to levels of risk and provides a focus on specific areas of risk within particular families.

Guide to the checklist

□indicates a level of risk. The more □ in a particular area the greater the level of risk

There is no critical number beyond which risk is unacceptable, but the more □ overall, the more likely it is that the issues of child protection are significant.

○ means there is no level of risk, or a low level of risk. The more ○ in a particular area, the more likely it is that risk in that area is low, or there is no risk.

There is no critical number below which no risk can be safely presumed, but the more ○, the more likely it is that issues of child protection are not significant.

△ means that insufficient information exists about the risks which may or may not exist. Further information is needed.

☆ means that risk exists at a significant level, or in a significant area. Professionals should consider that risk within the context of what intervention will safeguard and promote the welfare of the children.

Risk Indicator Checklist (RIC)

Name

Address

Family members

Person preparing RIC [name, designation and organisation]

Other professionals consulted [name, designation and organisation]

Length of involvement with child protection agencies

Information about the Family

	Yes	No	Don't know
Does the family feel isolated?	☐	○	△
Is the family targeted or exploited by the local community?	☐	○	△
Are there any neighbours or friends who offer positive support?	○	☐	△
Are family members supportive of each other?	○	☐	△
Is the family suffering from stress?	☐	○	△
Does the family have an adverse reaction to stress?	☐	○	△
Does the family present as disorganised?	☐	○	△
Are family routines child-centred?	○	☐	△
Has previous professional intervention resolved any of the above problems?	○	☐	△
Is the house dirty?	☐	○	△
Is the house cluttered with rubbish?	☐	○	△
Are there concerns about safety within the home?	☐	○	△
Have any agencies such as Environmental Health been involved?	☐	○	△
Has previous professional intervention resolved any of the above problems?	○	☐	△
Have professionals expressed concern recently?	☐	○	△
Has there been significant professional involvement?	☐	○	△
Have professionals ever felt intimidated?	☐	○	△
Have members of the family refused to work with professionals in the past?	☐	○	△

	Yes	No	Don't know
Has previous professional involvement resolved any of the above problems?	○	□	△
Does the family acknowledge any child protection concerns?	○	□	△
Is there evidence of violence within the family?	□	○	△
Are any children under 18 years of age living away from home?	□	○	△
Have children previously been removed from this family or from adults who are presently members of this family?	☆	○	△
Are any children being 'looked after' by the local authority?	☆	○	△
Have there been previous child protection concerns, including any investigations?	☆	○	△

Number of significant risk indicators   ☆ ___

Number of risk indicators   □ ___

Number of areas of non-indicated risk   ○ ___

Number of areas where insufficient information exists   △ ___

Information about Each of the Adults in the Home

Name

Relationship

	Yes	No	Don't know
Was s/he a victim of abuse as a child?	☐	○	△
Was the abuse over a long period?	☐	○	△
Did s/he witness abuse as a child?	☐	○	△
Did s/he witness family violence as a child?	☐	○	△
Did s/he have a difficult childhood?	☐	○	△
Was s/he in care?	☐	○	△
Did s/he have multiple carers as a child?	☐	○	△
Did s/he present difficult behaviour as a child?	☐	○	△
Did s/he present difficult behaviour as an adolescent?	☐	○	△
Has previous professional involvement resolved any of these issues?	○	☐	△
Is s/he under 18 years of age?	☐	○	△
Does s/he present difficult behaviours?	☐	○	△
Has s/he had employment difficulties?	☐	○	△
Is s/he unemployed?	☐	○	△
Has s/he a history of alcohol or drug abuse?	☐	○	△
Is the alcohol or drug abuse of long standing?	☐	○	△

	Yes	No	Don't know
Has s/he had failed attempts to detoxify?	☐	○	△
Are her/his friends also alcohol or drug abusers?	☐	○	△
Does s/he still abuse alcohol or drugs?	☐	○	△
Has s/he a history of serious mental health problems?	☐	○	△
Has s/he a personality disorder?	☐	○	△
Does s/he suffer from any degree of learning disability which could affect ability to care for children safely?	☐	○	△
Has s/he a history of violent behaviour within relationships?	☐	○	△
Has s/he ever been convicted of an offence of violence?	☐	○	△
Has s/he ever served a prison sentence for violence?	☐	○	△
Has s/he previously assaulted a child?	☆	○	△
Has s/he ever neglected or ill-treated a child in any way?	☆	○	△
Has s/he been a member of a household where a child has been neglected or ill-treated in any way?	☐	○	△
Are concerns held about her/his care of children?	☐	○	△
Does s/he place her/his own needs above those of children?	☐	○	△
Is there a lack of insight into the child's needs?	☐	○	△
Is there a failure to anticipate the child's needs?	☐	○	△
Is there a lack of concern for the child?	☐	○	△

	Yes	No	Don't know
Is there a lack of emotional warmth towards the child?	□	○	△
Does s/he have a poor child care focus?	□	○	△
Does s/he present a negative attitude to the child?	□	○	△
Does s/he scapegoat any of the children?	□	○	△
Does s/he have unrealistic expectations of the child?	□	○	△
Does s/he have poor knowledge about child care and child development?	□	○	△
Does her/his behaviour have a negative impact on the child?	□	○	△
Does s/he expose the child to the risk of significant harm?	☆	○	△
Number of significant risk indicators	☆	—	
Number of risk indicators	□	—	
Number of areas of non indicated risk	○	—	
Number of areas where insufficient information exists	△	—	

Information about Each Child

Name

Relationship

	Yes	No	Don't know
Was the child planned?	○	□	△
Was the child premature?	□	○	△
Were there any particular problems with the birth?	□	○	△
Was the child's birth weight low?	□	○	△
Is there any evidence of failure to thrive?	□	○	△
Does the child suffer from physical, sensory or learning disability?	□	○	△
Has the child reached her/his milestones?	○	■	△
Does the child have a history of multiple carers?	□	○	△
Is there a history of separation from parents?	□	○	△
Has the child had periods in care?	☆	○	△
Is there any evidence of attachment difficulties?	☆	○	△
Does the child's behaviour give cause for concern?	□	○	△
Has the child been frequently referred to the GP or hospital?	□	○	△
Have any referrals to the GP or hospital been inappropriate?	□	○	△
Is the child referred to by carers as being difficult, demanding, naughty, aggressive?	□	○	△

	Yes	No	Don't know
Is the child non-attending at school or arriving late for school?	☐	○	△
Is the child ever inappropriately dressed?	☐	○	△
Does the child ever look tired or neglected?	☐	○	△
Does the child have responsibilities beyond her/his age?	☐	○	△
Has the child ever been reported because of child protection concerns?	☆	○	△
Have other professionals expressed concern about the child's welfare?	☆	○	△
Has the child ever complained about the care received at home?	☆	○	△
Number of significant indicators	☆	___	
Number of risk indicators	☐	___	
Number of areas of non-indicated risk	○	___	
Number of areas where insufficient information exists	△	___	

1.3 THE CORE ASSESSMENT

The core assessment undertakes to establish a full understanding of the family to an extent that decisions can be made about:

- the extent of the risk to which the child(ren) are exposed

- the range of services needed to maintain the child(ren) within the family

- any action which is needed to safeguard and promote the welfare of the child(ren), including removal from the family.

In order to achieve this the tool uses processes for collecting information in a systematic way. These processes are designed to obtain core information and provide consistent quality of understanding of that information.

The tool also provides additional assessment material which can be used as appropriate for the specific needs of the family. For example, there is a guide for the assessment of family members where alcohol abuse may be a significant feature.

The assessment process

The assessment requires that all members of the family are assessed. It must take account of the unique characteristics of the family, and its accuracy depends upon good preparation, good observation and productive interviews.

The information required to assess children in need and their families is contained within the *Framework for the Assessment of Children in Need and their Families* (DoH 2000).

Preparation for the assessment

Before an assessment can begin the worker must prepare the order of the assessment, and in particular identify the specific areas of work to be undertaken.

There is a 'core' of information which is required and this is classified under the following headings:

- family structure

- chronology

- experiences from childhood

- perception of self

- perception of ideal self
- history of drugs/alcohol/significant issues
- criminal history
- health
- previous relationships
- present relationship
- parenting skills and abilities
- the home environment
- finances
- child care and child protection
- capacity to change.

When preparing for the assessment, the worker should look at what individual sessions should take place and the areas to be considered during each session. There is no prescription for the number of sessions, the length of the individual sessions, or the order in which the work is undertaken. However, it is essential to prepare an intended plan before commencing the work.

The length of sessions is important, especially with parents who may have a limited capacity to concentrate – for example, where learning disability is an issue. Workers need to remember that parents who become tired are unlikely to give a true picture of themselves, and the risk of alienation becomes real.

1.4 THE ASSESSMENT PLAN

The assessment plan should detail which of the sessions are to be undertaken jointly with the adults and which need to be individual. It may be appropriate to prepare the plan in consultation or conjunction with the family. In any event, the plan should be available for the family to agree.

The following issues should be included in a typical assessment plan:

Session 1	–	Chronology
Session 2	–	Chronology
Session 3	–	Experiences from childhood
Session 4	–	Experiences from childhood
Session 5	–	Perception of self and ideal self Violence, drugs, alcohol, criminal history, health
Session 6	–	Perception of self and ideal self Violence, drugs, alcohol, criminal history, health
Session 7	–	Previous relationships Perception of partner Relationship between adults
Session 8	–	Parenting skills and abilities
Session 9	–	Perception of the child(ren)
Session 10	–	Professional concerns
Session 11	–	Needs of the children
Session 12	–	Finances and home conditions
Session 13	–	Capacity to change

Where there are specific issues which give rise for concern – for example, violence or drug misuse – dedicated sessions may be necessary. Some sessions may overlap and it may be possible to incorporate some sessions together. Distress or upset may require some sessions to be ended prematurely, and others may be extended if the person is positively engaged. Therefore, whilst sessions should have a general time limit, flexibility is important. Workers should be alert to people, including themselves, becoming tired and losing concentration.

It is recommended that the following sessions should be conducted with each parent/person separately:

- perception of self
- perception of partner in the relationship section

- perception of the child(ren)

- parenting skills

- professional concerns.

If one of the adults prefers other sessions to be conducted separately this should be accommodated.

If a person requests or requires the support of a partner or other person for some or all of the sessions, this may have to be accommodated. However, the worker needs to take account of this in the evaluation, and to recognise the possibility that the information given is influenced by the presence of others. Any persons supporting another need to be aware that they should not interfere with the discussions or influence the person in any way.

Workers need to be careful if a dominant partner or parent insists on being present, and in exceptional circumstances exclusion may be essential to the assessment. It may be necessary to explain that information is only of value when it is not influenced in any way by others and therefore represents the true feelings of the person. For example discussing the perception of their partner with that person present is likely to influence the comments made. Some of the checklists depend upon the person not knowing what the other partner has written or said. Workers should negotiate with the adults and try to reach agreement, as this is more likely to maintain good relationships. There are some sessions – for example, chronology, education, and possibly experiences from childhood – which are less likely to be contaminated, as they are factual, and inclusion of the other person in these may allow agreement to be reached on them not attending other sessions. If negotiation and compromise fail, the worker may need to exercise some authority in ensuring that a position is established which enables the assessment to be properly completed.

Involvement of the family in the planning process should identify the precise arrangements for each session, and it is recommended that the issue of the support of partners/adults is resolved at this initial stage.

It is good practice to ensure that families from different ethnic backgrounds have representatives from those backgrounds as part of the assessment team, preferably involved in working directly with the family. This needs to be checked out with the family beforehand because of the possibility of any sensitivities. Where language is problematic, workers may need to recruit 'interpreters'. Only interpreters from approved organisations should be used, preferably with experience of working within the field of family assessment. Workers need to confirm that interpreters are familiar with any precise dialect the family uses, and are unrelated to the family, even through distant extended family.

Where other special arrangements are needed to facilitate the assessment – for example, assistance with sign language or Makaton sign language, or wheelchair access to buildings where assessment sessions are to take place – these should all be agreed in advance.

Time for observation should be included in the assessment, as this provides the opportunity to look at interactions and relationships. This 'space' is more easily achieved if there are two workers involved in the assessment.

Checklists which are going to be used with more than one member of the family should be given separately, and preferably within a time-scale which prevents them sharing information.

The venue for the assessment is important. In the main the work must be done in an environment where the family feels most comfortable. That would normally be the family home, and experience suggests that this is the setting in which many assessments can be undertaken. However, family homes can sometimes contain distractions and noise, which is unhelpful or even counterproductive. Some issues may be extremely sensitive, and the possibility of being overheard at home must be considered. There may be issues of safety for the workers which necessitate the work being undertaken in a setting where appropriate safeguards can be in place. Some sessions may need a specific setting, for example, a Family Centre to look at some practical parenting skills. Use of the family home and other settings may provide the most appropriate combination. It is most helpful to the assessment if at least one session can take place in the family home with all family members present, so that 'normal' family life can be observed.

The way in which these issues are negotiated and agreed with the family can often set the tone of the whole assessment. If the family feels marginalised or excluded from the process they may be resentful or resistant. The workers must ensure that the assessment is planned to ensure that the family is given every opportunity and is not 'set up' to fail.

1.5 INTRODUCING THE CASE STUDY

Case study personnel

David	–	subject
Michelle F	–	mother of David
Barry J	–	father of David
John B	–	Michelle's partner
Mr and Mrs K	–	John B's foster parents
Dianne A	–	previous partner of John B
Aimee A	–	daughter of John B and Dianne A
Annie M	–	Michelle's mother
Harry F	–	Michelle's birth father
George T	–	partner of Annie M
Bessie M	–	Michelle's maternal grandmother
Jack L	–	Michelle's half-brother
Alice L	–	wife of Jack
Janet S	–	social worker
Roger F	–	social worker
Jenny K	–	social work team leader

Michelle F is 26 years of age and has been known to social workers since she was seven years old. During her childhood the involvement was due to issues of general neglect. Michelle was reported to be a vulnerable child.

There was a child protection case conference when Michelle was 11 years old, which concluded that there was insufficient evidence to remove her from home, but significant concerns were expressed about the poor levels of care afforded to her.

A child protection investigation occurred when Michelle was 15 years old and had been 'over-chastised' by her mother. Consideration was given to care proceedings and removal from home, but Michelle wanted to remain in the family so 'she could look after her grandmother, who was at the time recovering from a serious illness'.

When Michelle was 22 years old she became pregnant and a pre-birth case conference was held. It was decided that the child's name should be placed on the Child Protection Register at birth. Michelle agreed to go and live with her grandmother, and on the basis of a signed agreement to that effect, the baby, David, was allowed to remain in her care.

Despite some concerns, David generally thrived. It was accepted that the grandmother provided for most of David's primary care needs.

A nursery place was made available for David, when he was two years old, as part of the family support package, and this was increased from time to time to respond to the needs of the family.

At the nursery, David presented as a lively little boy who was developing within normal limits. Michelle was seen to be anxious about David and required constant reassurance. She had difficulty managing him and he showed aggressive behaviour with her which was not apparent elsewhere. Nursery staff felt that Michelle was isolated and lonely. Michelle was described as being overly reliant on her grandmother and demonstrated few parental skills and abilities.

David's father is Barry J. He is 36 years of age. Michelle was not supported by David's father. He is described as a vulnerable adult who lives with his parents and is dependent on them for much of his day-to-day requirements.

Michelle met John B and began living with him the same day. John B was 42, and not previously known to the social services department in Newton. He revealed information about previous convictions which gave rise for concern. When David and Michelle went to live with John B, a further case conference was convened. The conference was told that Michelle was alienated from her family and there were concerns about the physical conditions in which David was living. However, it was agreed that David should be allowed to remain in the care of his mother and her partner John, and that support should be offered to the family while a core assessment was completed.

From the outset, John B refused social workers admission to the house, alleging that they were interfering in his life. This prevented the assessment being completed. David stopped attending nursery once

John became involved, and this caused concern as it had been one of the main opportunities for monitoring David.

A case conference was about to be convened when, on 24 August, Newton General Hospital referred David to the social services department. He had arrived at the hospital in a taxi, with his mother. A little while later, the mother's partner had arrived, apparently drunk or under the influence of drugs.

The explanation given by the mother was that David had fallen from a chair and banged his arm. X-rays revealed two fractures to the right arm. They were thought to have occurred at separate times because of the different levels of healing. A leg fracture was also discovered, and this was very recent. There were two healing blisters on David's buttocks which could possibly have been cigarette burns, but this was not conclusive. A full skeletal survey revealed a number of healed rib fractures. David was described as withdrawn and fearful, his expression one of 'frozen awareness'. He told hospital staff that he had fallen.

When informed that non-accidental injury was suspected, John B became aggressive and threatening. He left the hospital when the police were contacted by hospital staff.

Michelle F was described as stunned and tearful. She agreed to David being accommodated under the Children Act 1989. Care proceedings were immediately commenced.

David remained in hospital for six days and was transferred to foster carers.

An expert opinion was sought from a paediatric radiologist who concluded:

> David is 4 years old. The fractures are of different ages and this is suspicious. There are at least four traumatic episodes, none of which would have occurred as a result of the explanations given by the parents. The arm fractures in particular show evidence of a twisting aspect which would not be seen in an accidental fall.
>
> In my opinion, considerable intentional force would be required. It is my conclusion that the subject has been non-accidentally injured.

A child protection case conference registered David's name under the category of 'actual physical harm'. It was concluded that a core assessment was needed.

1.6 THE ASSESSMENT AGREEMENT

The assessment plan leads to the preparation of an assessment agreement, which should be prepared in conjunction with the family. This agreement informs the assessment process. It is designed to provide each of the parties with an understanding of all of the elements of the assessment. It should explain what will happen and when. Workers must recognise that, whilst to them the assessment is something familiar, to families it is a completely new, frightening and threatening experience. For them the possible disintegration of their family is at stake.

Preparing such an agreement with the family before the assessment begins prevents confusion about dates, times, etc. It also includes the family as part of the process and is therefore more likely to encourage their support and co-operation. Workers should attempt to reassure the family as much as possible and should be prepared to include issues which are important to the family. Families must not, however, be made promises or given false optimism in order to encourage co-operation.

In looking at the dates and times of assessment sessions, account should be taken of the family's routines and commitments – for example, collecting children from school, or times of religious observance – and these should be accommodated. Family should not be asked to take time off work to attend assessment sessions, unless that is unavoidable.

However, assessment sessions should not be designed around routines which can temporarily be set aside to accommodate the assessment. For example, it might be reasonable to expect a family member to sacrifice the weekly 'game of snooker with the lads' in order to attend sessions.

In the same way, workers have to be flexible and responsive. Assessments cannot always be completed Monday to Friday, 9.00am to 5.00pm, nor would it be appropriate for that to be the framework. Families who are seen at different times of the day, in different conditions and different settings, will usually provide a more comprehensive picture for the workers.

An assessment agreement should:

- explain the reason for the assessment
- establish the responsibilities of the workers
- establish the responsibilities of the parents, children and any other persons
- note the sessions, including dates, times, venues and any special arrangements

- specify arrangements for the cancellation of sessions
- provide a time-scale for the assessment
- explain how disputes and disagreements will be resolved
- identify contingency arrangements
- describe what will happen to the assessment.

Case study

The Assessment Agreement

Agreement between Newton Social Services Department and Michelle F and John B.

Reason for the assessment

This assessment is being undertaken because Michelle's son, David, has been injured and doctors at the hospital have said that it could not have happened in the way that Michelle and her partner John have explained. They say that someone has injured David.

Michelle and John deny that they have done anything which could have caused these injuries to David. They say they have never hurt David in any way.

At the moment David is being accommodated with the agreement of Michelle, who is the only person with parental responsibility. Michelle has agreed to allow David to remain with foster carers until the assessment is completed.

Time-scale for the assessment

The assessment will be completed by [date]

What the workers undertaking the assessment will do

Janet S and Roger F will be responsible for the assessment.

Janet will undertake the sessions with Michelle.

Roger will undertake the sessions with John.

Janet and Roger will meet together with Michelle and John for joint sessions.

Janet will ensure that David is brought to the Family Centre for the family sessions.

Roger will ensure that Michelle and John are transported to the Family Centre for sessions when this has been agreed.

Janet and Roger will reimburse travel costs where that is needed.

If Janet or Roger have to cancel any sessions, they will rearrange dates and agree these with Michelle and John. They will amend this agreement and initial the changes, or send a letter to confirm the changes.

Changes will only be made for valid reasons.

Janet and Roger will tell Michelle and John as soon as possible if sessions have to be cancelled.

Janet and Roger will rearrange any sessions which Michelle or John cancel for a valid reason.

Sessions will be cancelled if John is under the influence of drugs or alcohol.

If John becomes angry during any of the sessions, workers will suggest a short break.

Sessions will be stopped if John threatens staff or if he remains angry.

What the parents / adults / child(ren) will do

Michelle and John will attend all of the agreed sessions on time or be ready when transport arrives to collect them.

Michelle and John will only cancel sessions if there is a good reason.

If John becomes angry during any of the sessions, he will ask for a short break.

If sessions have to be cancelled, Michelle or John will ensure that someone lets the area office know as soon as possible.

John will not attend any of the sessions under the influence of drugs or alcohol.

Assessment sessions (example)

Session 6

Date and time:	10 Jan. 2002 10.00am
Venue:	Family home
People to attend:	Michelle, John, Janet and Roger
Topic:	Relationship, Michelle and John

What about complaints and disagreements?

If either Michelle and John, or Janet and Roger have a complaint, this will be looked at first by Jenny K, the workers' manager. If it cannot be resolved by her, and the assessment cannot continue, a case conference will be held. Michelle and John will be invited to that meeting.

Contingency arrangements

If the assessment is not completed, or is stopped by either the family or the workers, a case conference will be called immediately to decide what will happen.

At all times David must be protected from the risk of significant harm, and action will be taken to ensure this.

What will happen to the assessment

The completed assessment will be discussed with Michelle and John and after the contents have been discussed they will be given a copy.

Any disagreements they have will be recorded at the end of the assessment.

The assessment will be considered at the child protection case conference on [date] That conference will decide what happens next.

Signed   ....   Date   ....
[Michelle]

Signed [John]   ....   Date   ....

Signed [Janet] ....   Date   ....

Signed [Roger] ....   Date   ....

1.7 THE ASSESSMENT INTERVIEWS

Before any assessment work is undertaken the worker should identify the following issues in respect of the family members, and they must be resolved to the satisfaction of all concerned:

- ability to read and write
- level of understanding
- particular difficulties – for example, dyslexia
- issues of race, culture, and religion which must be accommodated
- difficulties where English is not the family's first language.

Where the ability to read or write is limited, the worker should ensure that account is taken of this in the sessions. Where written material is being used, the worker should read it to the family member and record the responses.

Where levels of understanding are limited – for example, by learning disability – workers should use only words which the person understands (simple rather than complex language). Regular checks should be made to ensure that the person understands the issues being discussed.

Learning-disabled adults, and younger children, are more likely to need and request the presence of a supporter during sessions, and this should be respected. There is often a balance between the potential influence and interference of a supporter and the benefits gained when a person/child feels more relaxed, and therefore more likely to engage with the worker.

Workers should ensure that issues of language, culture, ethnic background, disability, sexuality, gender, or any other significant issues are accommodated. If they are not, the assessment is likely to be confronted with them at some stage and this could disrupt the assessment or even prevent its completion. The more issues are resolved before the assessment begins, the more likely it is that matters will progress satisfactorily.

If translators are necessary, they should be from an independent translator service, not family members. Whenever possible, they should be experienced in this type of work, or at least familiar with what is likely to be encountered and what will be expected of them. Workers should meet with the interpreter before the assessment begins. Ways of working should be examined and the interpreter should be clear about roles, styles of working and how questions will be asked. The interpreter's preferred way of translating should be accommodated if that is possible. For example, some interpreters are able to translate long sentences, while others prefer sentences to be broken down into brief sections. Workers should make it clear that a precise translation is needed at all times. If, for any reason, words or sentences are not understood by the interpreter, s/he should inform the worker immediately. Workers should be alert to how tired the interpreter is becoming. Breaks should be accommodated. The assessment process/sessions may need to be reviewed in the light of issues/difficulties which early sessions identify.

The family should be encouraged to ask for questions or comments to be repeated if they do not understand. Workers should never use professional terminology or jargon. Family members who do not understand questions may either become frustrated or disengage from the assessment process. People who feel they are being patronised or 'talked down to' are likely to be angry or feel that decisions have already been made. All of these responses are likely to contaminate the accuracy of the assessment.

Workers need to acknowledge with families that the assessment is an invasion into their lives. A significant amount of time will be spent with them in a relatively short time-scale. Family routines and systems are likely to be disrupted and family members inconvenienced by the process.

Workers also need to acknowledge with families that some issues discussed may cause them upset/distress/anger, etc., and that most of these are 'normal' responses in this situation. Workers should share with the person/family their recognition of this. Apologising for any distress which is likely to be caused is, in many instances, positively received and helps to engage the family. Workers will probably be able to anticipate sessions which are going to be difficult for people, and to prepare by, for example, having planned breaks, or having someone available who will be able to provide appropriate support.

Each interview should have a clear focus on the topic for the session, for example, the person's perception of themselves. This will be identified in the assessment plan which has been agreed with the family.

Before each interview the worker should plan the issues to be covered in the session and collect together any necessary materials, for example, large sheets of paper for chronologies or family trees. Checklists which will be required should be made ready, and the worker should study them to identify dedicated areas of focus or add their own specific issues to those already provided in the checklist.

Where sessions are being conducted with another worker, roles and responsibilities should be agreed. If this is not done, confusion and lack of understanding are likely to result. This leads to unsatisfactory sessions and will probably affect the quality of the assessment.

The person or persons to be involved in the session should be aware of the issues to be discussed and invited, where that is appropriate, to consider the issues in advance.

Checklists and 'homework' completed by members of the family in advance of sessions are never recommended, even where time-scales are very short. Any work undertaken out of sight of the worker risks contamination by others, and is therefore best avoided. It cannot be relied upon to the same extent. Out-of-sight preparation of information by family can be considered where factual information is being collected, for example, family structures or criminal history. Spot checks on that information, for example, by asking for clarification on a specific event, are likely to confirm authenticity.

Assessment sessions require the detailed recording of information. Families can find this process intimidating. Difficulties and concerns can be overcome if families are offered access to, or copies of, the notes taken. Similarly, some workers tape-record assessment sessions. Access to, or copies of, the tapes should be offered. Where the assessment is being undertaken jointly, it may be appropriate for one worker to ask the questions and the other to write down the answers.

Assessment is not only the process of asking questions and analysing information. The observation of behaviour, actions, reactions and interactions is equally important, and workers should be alert to this at all times.

Families often ask for instant feedback from sessions. It is helpful for workers to look at how they will deal with this. A neutral response is usually the most helpful way forward, as it keeps the family engaged in the assessment. Inviting the family to comment on how they feel the assessment is going can embroil workers in discussions which may not produce an ongoing engagement, and is usually best avoided. It is often possible to comment that, until all of the assessment sessions are completed, a comment on progress or outcome is not helpful.

Wherever possible, questions should be open-ended and so require a narrative response from the person. In this way the worker says less and family members say more. For example, if a family member is asked 'do you become angry often?', they will answer either 'Yes' or 'No'. The worker is then required to ask further questions in order to receive more information. In addition, posed a question which requires such a response, the person is more likely to provide an answer which will both reflect them in a good light and help them to achieve a positive assessment. The open-ended question approach encourages description, rather than a one-word answer. For example, if the question is, 'How often do you become angry?' the person is more likely to provide a narrative response, which will be more informative. The interview then becomes more of a discussion than a question-and- answer session. Direct questions should only be considered as a follow-up to the person's initial response or if a specific response is required.

Some of the checklists do require specific 'yes/no' responses, for example, the risk indicator checklist. This is because these checklists are designed to look at balancing positive and negative aspects of a particular area of behaviour, relationship or family dynamic.

In using the open-ended approach to questions, a sequence should be used. For example, when looking at the issue of anger, the following sequence of questions might be asked.

- What things make you angry?

The worker then waits for the person to list the things which cause anger. Where clarification is needed to any of the answers, it is sought. For example if the person replies, 'people who interfere', the worker might want to explore further by asking as a subsidiary question, 'Who are the people who interfere who make you angry?' or 'In what ways do people interfere that make you angry?' In some situations both subsidiary questions may be appropriate. The worker then moves on to:

- When was the last time you were angry and what happened?

- Describe the most angry you have ever been in your life and what happened?

- How often do you feel angry?

- How do you feel when you are angry?

- What do you normally do when you are angry?

- What do you do to try and control your anger?

- Would you like to be angry more often or less often?

Optional specific questions which may be asked, if not answered in the free narrative above, are:

- Would you like to control your anger more?

- Are you angry more often now than when you were younger?

- Are there specific people who make you angry?

- Are there specific situations which make you angry?

Finally, questions which relate to known information can be asked:

- You lost your temper with your partner last week, could you tell me about that?

1.8 THE FIRST ASSESSMENT SESSION

The first session sets the tone for all subsequent sessions and it is important that it is as positive as possible. Generally a person's chronology, whilst perhaps upsetting in parts for the person, is not contentious, and so is unlikely to cause difficulties between the person and the worker. Therefore, not only is it an obvious place, but also an appropriate place to start.

Before beginning anything, however, the worker needs to establish that the arrangements for the assessment are agreed. Where no assessment agreement has been made – for example, where an independent social worker has been commissioned, or where time-scales are very short – the assessment process should be explained, and the dates of sessions agreed. The family should be invited to ask any questions and identify any concerns they have.

The importance of the family and workers being truthful and honest with each other needs to be stressed. Factual information which is given but which is not true, or information which is withheld, for example, a criminal conviction, is likely to discredit what might be an otherwise honest account, or to contaminate an otherwise positive assessment.

Achieving a positive climate for the assessment is more likely if:

- family members are treated with respect and courtesy at all times

- workers use positive body language, and avoid negative body language, at all times

- negative responses, such as head-shaking, are avoided.

- the views and opinions of the family are received in a neutral and non-judgemental way

- family members are made to feel involved

- workers present themselves professionally

- furniture, for example, a table, is not used as a barrier.

1.9 ASSESSING THE PARENTS

The assessment of the parents is obtained through a complete understanding of all aspects of their life history, their experiences, perceptions, concepts, relationships, abilities and skills, attitudes and belief systems. It is a complex process which requires a systematic method of collecting the information, and this is why this tool uses checklists. Checklists ensure that nothing is missed.

The following areas are explored in order to provide a core assessment of the adults involved:

- a comprehensive account of their life experiences

- the perceptions they have

- their past and present relationships

- their abilities and skills

- their strengths and weaknesses

- their capacity to make changes.

In order to achieve this core understanding, it will be necessary to explore with them:

- an understanding of their family

- an understanding of how they grew up

- their experiences in childhood

- the perception they have about themselves

- the perceptions they have about others

- the kind of parent they are

- the kind of parent they are capable of being.

CHAPTER 2

Collecting the Data
for Assessment

2.1 THE FAMILY STRUCTURE

Whilst some workers prefer to compile a family tree to include information as far back as family members can remember, this tool recommends compiling family tree information as far back as the child(ren)'s grandparents. Information which is significant beyond that will be collected within the 'experiences from childhood' section.

Some family members prefer to talk about their parents and siblings whilst others prefer to draw, or have drawn for them, a family tree. The choice should be offered.

Where the family tree is preferred, the family member should be offered the choice of either completing it him/herself, or providing the information to the worker to compile. If the worker is compiling the family tree, the family member should be able to see the chart at all times. Workers can use this checklist selectively.

When exploring family composition, account should be taken of feelings which may arise when those being assessed talk about family members who are deceased. The person's emotions and distress should be responded to appropriately.

The family structure checklist

- What is his/her name?

- How does he/she prefer to be known?

- How old is he/she?

- Where does he/she live?

- Who does he/she currently live with?

- How often do you see him/her?

- What is your current relationship with him/her?

- Have social workers ever been involved with him/her? If so how, in what way and what happened?

Case study

Michelle's family

Michelle is the only child of Annie M and Harry F.

Her mother lives at 12 Low Street, Newton, with her partner George T. Michelle does not speak to her mother and describes their relationship as 'non-existent'. They sometimes meet accidentally in town, but according to Michelle, they ignore each other. Michelle refers to George T as her father although biologically that is not the case.

Michelle has never met her birth father and does not know where he lives. Michelle has asked her mother about her birth father on a number of occasions but the information has always been refused.

She was told by her maternal grandmother, Bessie M, that her father ran off to Whattown with another woman before Michelle was born.

Michelle has a half-brother, Jack L, who is 22 years old. He lives with his partner, Alice L, at 14 Back Lane, Newton. They have two sons, John L, aged 6, and Paul L, aged 4. Michelle sees Jack from time to time when they 'bump into each other'. Michelle says that Jack is 'a bit slow', and thinks that social workers keep threatening to take his children from him because he drinks a lot and the children are not fed properly. Michelle feels they get on okay and that she likes him sometimes.

John's family

John has no living family members of whom he is aware. He does not know the names of his birth parents. He prefers it like that.

Training exercise/case study

There is a case study which looks at the family structure in the Appendix, Exercise 1.

2.2 CHRONOLOGY

The chronology records the person's life from birth to the present time. It does not need to dwell on minute detail, perceptions or feelings, as the important features will be obtained in subsequent sessions. As with all aspects of the assessment, it must go at a pace with which the person feels comfortable. The worker must respect the person's right to explain their life in their way.

A detailed understanding of the person's childhood and adult life is required because the experiences which people have provides workers with clues and information about their present skills, abilities, knowledge and understanding. Attitudes and beliefs are frequently rooted in childhood experiences. It is important for the worker to have examined all available case history information, as this will act as a cross-reference for the information provided. It will also assist in examining some of the issues with the person.

Workers must be sensitive to the difficulties which some people have when recounting their background. Be prepared to allow for 'time out' if the person becomes distressed, and be appropriately supportive of them. Acknowledge how difficult recalling some of the information might be, and reassure them that to record their recollections and memories is more important than being entirely accurate about, for example, the date of particular events.

If the worker anticipates that the session will be difficult for the person, arrangements should be made to have a family member, friend or professional available to support them immediately after the session has ended.

Throughout this and all the sessions the worker must provide a climate which enables the information to be collected and which encourages the person's feelings, views and opinions to be expressed.

The non-directive approach which is used allows the person to recall their childhood and memories in their own way and in their own words. Gaps in the information can be clarified subsequently. Note should be taken of what is *not* reported during this free rapport phase. Information may have been forgotten, blocked or deliberately withheld.

Workers should allow for silences during the person's report. 'Moving on' or 'moving in' may inhibit the person's account. Silences allow them the opportunity to continue their account.

Workers can use the following checklist selectively.

Checklist on chronology

- Where were you born?

- What is the first thing you can remember?

- What else do you remember?

- And then what?

Limiting the questions in this way encourages the person to think about what they can remember. It allows them to report their version of their childhood and adult life. If the person finds it difficult to begin, remember or report their memories, some prompting questions may help.

- Do you remember any of your brothers or sisters being born?

- Do you remember starting school?

- Do you remember? (mention a significant known incident in the person's childhood)

These questions give a reference to the person's age at the time and allow a re-focus on the memories.

Once the person has reported their childhood and adult life, the worker may want to re-focus on events which have been missed and discuss these. Information from case files and case histories will assist with this. For instance the person may have omitted to report a period 'in care', and this can be explored.

Case Study

Michelle's chronology

Michelle was born in Newton. She thinks that her mother was in labour for a long time and she was born with the cord around her neck.

She was brought up by her mother and grandmother until she was four years old. Her mother then met George T and they moved into his house at 28 Back Lane, Newton.

Michelle's first memory is of being taken to school by her grandmother. She is not clear how old she was but thinks it might have been when she was five.

She remembers sleeping at her grandmother's house for a period when her half-brother Jack was born.

When she was eleven years of age, Michelle was involved in an accident. She was knocked down by a car whilst playing in the street. She broke her leg in three places and was an in-patient in hospital for two months. Michelle remembers her grandmother visiting but does not remember her mother and step-father coming to see her.

When she was twelve years old, George T was made redundant and the family moved in to live with her grandmother. Michelle thinks they stayed there for about a year.

The family then returned to Back Lane to live at number 46. Michelle remembers playing on the street by herself because no-one else would play with her. The other children used to call her names and hit her. She told her mother once but was smacked and told to stick up for herself.

After she left school, Michelle went to Newton College to continue to improve her reading and writing and help to prepare her for getting work, but she did not like that very much.

For a little while she was at home with nothing to do, so she started going to the Willows Centre. She described this as a place where people could go. Staff were around and she could talk to them about how she was feeling and discuss any problems she might have. They showed her how to cook things and helped with her reading and writing.

Michelle met Barry J at the centre when she was 22 years old. They have a son, David, who is four years old. After David was born, Michelle went to live with her grandmother.

Barry J used to see David each week when he visited Michelle's grandmother. According to Michelle this worked reasonably well until she started living with John B. Since that time Barry has refused to have anything to do with his son.

Michelle continued to live with her grandmother until about eight months ago, which was when she met John B. According to Michelle, they got on really well immediately. She thinks she moved into his flat a few days after they met.

Michelle explained that it was more difficult looking after David when her grandmother was not there to help.

On 26 June 2000 her grandmother died of a heart attack. Michelle felt devastated by this.

On 24 August 2000 Michelle took David to her mother because he seemed to be 'walking badly'. Her mother said she could not help and told Michelle to take David to the doctor, which she did. The doctor called an ambulance and he was taken to hospital.

After a few days in hospital he was placed with foster carers. Michelle agreed to this. She thinks that she signed some forms to say that it was okay. Michelle currently lives with her partner John at his flat, 39 Front Terrace, Newton.

John's chronology

John has been told that he was born in London and abandoned by his mother at a very early age.

His first memory is at the Larches Children's Home. He believes that this was around the time that he started school.

He remembers being made to stand outside with his bedding which he had soiled during the night. He has vague memories of being cold and wet.

When John was six years old he was placed with foster carers for six months and then transferred to another set of foster carers when the placement broke down.

He remained with these carers until he was eleven years of age. The placement ended when the foster mother died suddenly.

John returned to the Larches Children's Home, but did not like it and began to run away on a regular basis. Around this time he also started breaking into cars and committing other offences. There was a group of older young people in the children's home and John became a member of that gang.

When he was approximately thirteen-and-a-half years of age John was placed at the Beeches Unit. John described this placement as one made completely without warning and preparation. The Beeches was hundreds of miles away from his home. He recalls feelings of anger and distress at what was happening to him. He was unable to settle at the Beeches and became a persistent absconder. He would often steal cars in order to aid his return home.

John was then placed in a number of different residential units miles away from home, and eventually he was placed in secure accommodation. He was there for approximately six months and described it as one of the most settled periods of his childhood.

On his release from secure accommodation, John refused to return to live at the Larches Children's Home and was therefore placed in bed and breakfast accommodation.

He quickly became involved in further offending behaviour, and on his sixteenth birthday he was placed at a young offenders institution where he remained for two years.

He found it impossible to settle once he was released and for several years he travelled around the country.

He became heavily involved in the drug scene, and 'several years went by in a bit of a haze'.

During this period, John met Dianne A. Dianne had two children, Claire, aged four, and Darren, aged two, and they were living in privately rented accommodation in Fartown. Dianne was using heroin.

John and Dianne remained together for about five years, although during that period they both served prison sentences.

When Dianne was first imprisoned, Claire and Darren went to live with Dianne's parents and remained there after she was released. Dianne and John had a girl, Aimee, who was born 12 September 1994.

According to John, they looked after Aimee for a few weeks and then she also went to live with Dianne's parents. This was after the social services department had become involved.

Shortly after Aimee went to live with her grandparents, John was sent to prison again. He reported that whilst in prison he withdrew from drugs and when he was released he decided to 'make a fresh start', and moved to Newton.

Initially he lived at a hostel for the homeless and then obtained his own flat. He met Michelle when he was out one night and they started living together fairly soon thereafter.

Training exercise/case study

There is a case study looking at chronology in the Appendix, Exercise 2.

2.3 EXPERIENCES FROM CHILDHOOD

Once a chronology has been obtained, the worker should return to the person's childhood and look in more detail at experiences and perceptions. The person should be encouraged to talk about their childhood rather than provide short responses to questions. Ask subsidiary questions, where the person makes comments which need clarification. For example, if they say that they felt really unhappy most of the time up to being ten years of age, this should be further explored as it is likely to provide significant understanding of their emotional well-being at that time.

Explore with the person comments they make which might give insight into their experiences. For example, 'I was treated differently from my brothers and sisters.' Explore examples of this, which might give clues to:

- whether the treatment was different

- whether or not the person's perception is distorted i.e. the treatment was the same and the perception is wrong

- to what extent that affected the care the person received

- how the person feels about that now

- if the treatment was different, what would the person do to avoid that with their children?

The person's perception of each adult who played an important part in their lives helps to gain a full understanding of the level of care they received and also what they learned about being a parent from these people. Workers should first of all list the adults whom the person remembers as being important to them – 'important' because of good memories and bad memories.

Use this checklist selectively.

Checklist for experiences from childhood

In respect of each parent and any adult who was important to the person or played a significant part in their life:

- Describe your father/mother/important person.

- Say three good things about them.

- Say three bad things about them.

- Did they go out to work when you were a child?

- How long did you live with them?

- What do you remember as the thing you liked most about them?

- What do you remember as the thing you liked least about them?
- Did they have any particular difficulties when you were growing up (for example, alcohol abuse)?
- What kind of things did you do together?
- What would they do if you were naughty?
- What did they consider was naughty enough to be punished?
- How often did they punish you?
- What was the worst punishment you ever received from them?
- Were you ever punished when you felt you did not deserve it?
- Did you get hugs and cuddles from them?
- How often did you get hugs and cuddles?
- Describe your relationship with them now.

About the relationship of the person's parents/primary carers:

- What kind of relationship do you think they had?
- How well do you think they got on together?
- Was either person in charge of the relationship? If so, why do you think that was?
- How often did they argue?
- What kind of things did they argue about?
- What happened when they argued?
- Who came off best when they argued?
- Were they ever violent to each other?
- How did you feel when they argued or were violent?
- Why do you think they behaved in the way they did?

In respect of each sibling, step-sibling or half-sibling:

- How would you describe them?
- What did you like most about them?
- What did you like least about them?
- Describe your relationship with them.

- How much time did you spend together, playing or doing things?
- What things did you do together?
- What was the worst thing they ever did to you?
- What was the worst thing you ever did to them?
- What was the nicest thing they ever did to you/for you?
- What was the nicest thing you ever did to them/for them?
- How would you describe your relationship with them now?
- Describe any ways in which you were treated differently by your parents.

Perception of home:

- Describe your home as you were growing up. What was it like?
- Who lived there?
- Where did everyone sleep?
- Describe the kind of meals you had.
- Describe the kind of clothes you wore.
- Would you say your family was poor or well off?

Perceptions of self in childhood :

- What kind of child do you think you were?
- What was the happiest time in your childhood?
- What was the unhappiest time in your childhood?
- What was the naughtiest thing you ever did?
- Describe something in your childhood which made you feel really proud.
- Describe times in your childhood when someone really hurt you.
- Describe things from your childhood which still upset you.
- Tell me about anything or anyone who made you feel afraid.

Relationship with local community:

- What was the area like where you were brought up?

- What kind of things did you do for play?

- Who did you play with?

- Describe any time when people picked on your family.

- Tell me about times when members of the family were called names.

- How would you describe your home?

Overall perceptions:

- What kind of childhood do you think you had?

- Describe three good things and three bad things from your childhood.

- If you could have changed anything about your childhood, what would it have been?

- What do you think you have learned from your childhood about yourself?

- In what ways do you think you take after either of your parents?

- What do you think you learned from childhood about being a parent yourself?

- What support does your family currently provide for you?

Case study

Michelle's experiences from childhood

Michelle described her mother in the following terms:

'Nice...in her own way.'

'She used to drink a lot...she still does.'

'She can cook.'

'When she lost her temper you had to watch out.'

'She would stand up for herself.'

'Fat.'

'She never loved me properly...neither of them did.'

'She would go out to the pub and leave us alone in the house.'

When the comment about temper was explored, Michelle reported that when her mother lost her temper she would hit her and her brother with anything she could get her hands on. Jack and she would try to run round to their maternal grandmother, who could stop their mother hitting them.

Michelle's mother remained at home to look after them. She had an evening cleaning job once but that did not last very long.

Her mother's best feature was, 'She gave us money when she was drunk,' and she least liked her mother, 'When she lost her temper, which was most of the time'.

Michelle does not remember doing things with her mother. They did go on holiday to the seaside once but she thinks that was with her grandmother.

Michelle does not feel she was naughty when she was a child. However, her mother often said she had been, and Michelle remembers being sent to bed without any tea. She remembers her mother hitting her for no reason, and once she received a cut on her head when her mother threw something at her. The worst punishment she ever received was when she was hit on her bottom with her father's leather belt after she had knocked over her mother's bottle of sherry. She was told at the time never to tell anyone about what had happened.

She does not remember going to her mother for comfort. The only time her mother cuddled and kissed her was when she had been drinking, and Michelle reported feeling afraid to go to her mother because sometimes she was cuddled and other times she was hit.

Michelle is alienated from her mother at present and has been since she met John. She explained that John and her mother hated each other from the start.

Michelle has never met her birth father and recognises George T as her father. She described him in the following terms:

'He used to sulk a lot.'

'He was always shouting at me.'

'He used to shout at my mother when she was drunk.'

'He has a nasty streak.'

'He could be funny sometimes...but it never lasted.'

'He was better before he lost his job.'

Michelle felt that her father used to shout at Jack just as much as he did at her.

She described the nicest thing about him as, 'nothing really...he was all right when we were small', and she liked him least 'when he shouted'.

Michelle never did anything with her father.

He only ever smacked her if her mother was not at home to do it. He did not smack her for 'little things like my mother did', but when he did smack her it really hurt.

He once made Michelle wash her mouth out with soap after she had sworn. Michelle still feels aggrieved about this as he swears all the time. She has always wanted to tell him but has not been able to do so.

Michelle reported that she was never once hugged by him.

She thinks that she would like to speak to her father but she knows that John would be really angry with her.

Michelle feels that her grandmother was really important to her and she was devastated when she died recently. She described her in the following terms:

'Kind.'

'She used to play with me because no-one else would.'

'She baked really delicious cakes.'

'I loved her.'

Michelle felt she could always go to her grandmother when she was upset. She always had sweets in the cupboard and Jack and Michelle would go round to see her as often as they could.

Michelle remembers being really upset when she was twelve years old and her mother stopped speaking to 'Gran'. This meant they could no longer visit her.

Michelle remembers that her parents were always either arguing or not speaking to each other. She does not recall a time when they got on well. Her mother was the one who did the work around the house and cooked the meals, although they never had a lot to eat. Sometimes she and Jack would sit at the top of the stairs and listen to them fighting. This made Michelle feel really frightened. Her mother and father often hit each other.

Michelle thinks they behaved like this because 'that's how they are …they will never change…people never do'. Michelle had heard her grandmother say that once and she agrees.

Michelle thinks she got on okay with her brother Jack. They used to play together sometimes, but mainly he was out with his friends and she was at home by herself.

They used to hit each other sometimes but nothing serious ever happened. When this was explored Michelle said that nobody ever ended up in hospital.

He once bought her a doll for her birthday, which she loved.

She does not feel very close to Jack now, particularly since he met Alice L. At present she does not like him because his children are still at home and she looked after David much better than they look after their kids.

Michelle liked the area where she was brought up, although she did not like most of the people because they picked on her and called her names.

Their house was 'scruffy' and there was nowhere to play except the street, which Michelle avoided because of the other children.

Michelle thinks that her childhood was good. She believes that her parents loved her and cared for her properly. She would not want to have changed anything, except she would have liked her grandmother to have lived with them because she would have stopped her mother and father fighting.

She thinks her parents were good and she would like to be as good a parent herself.

She learned that children should be loved instead of smacked, she thinks that is very important. She also learned that when parents fight, the children are frightened. She would not want any of her children to be frightened.

If David came back to live with them she would ask John if she could speak to her mother and father again.

John's experiences from childhood

John has never met either of his birth parents. He was brought up in a variety of different care settings, most of them short-term, and none within which John felt settled or happy.

There was a period from six years to eleven years when he lived with Mr and Mrs K, who were local authority approved foster carers. John was able to acknowledge that this was a time in his childhood when he felt reasonably settled and contented.

John described Mrs K in the following terms:

'She was okay.'

'She used to shout at me if I was naughty but she never hit me once.'

'She once stuck up for me when I was in trouble at school.'

'She was probably the nearest thing to a mother I have ever had.'

John remembers being told off by the foster mother if he was naughty and sometimes he was sent to his room. However, he was never hit whilst he was in this placement.

He does remember that the foster mother used to tuck him up in bed, and she would often sit and talk to him whilst he was going to sleep. Even if he soiled himself during the night, she did not shout at him.

Mr K was a long-distance lorry driver and therefore spent lots of time away from home. However, he was generally home at weekends and John remembers that they used to go shopping together and he would be allowed to help choose what they were going to have to eat the following week. Mr K was keen on football and on a Saturday afternoon they would sometimes go and watch Fairtown United. John was allowed to sit on Mr K's shoulders so that he could see the match.

They had two grown-up daughters who used to visit quite frequently.

John does not remember Mr and Mrs K arguing very much, he does remember they used to 'laugh a lot and act daft', which used to make him laugh.

John was devastated when Mrs K died suddenly. He remembers being collected from school by a social worker and taken to the Larches Children's Home instead of to the foster home. For a long time he thought it was because he had done something wrong, but eventually one of the staff at the Larches told him that the foster mother had died.

He remembers feeling very angry when he was told about Mrs K's death, he sat in his room and cried for ages, but nobody came to comfort him.

John described Mr K in the following terms:

'He was big and cuddly and always laughing.'

'He had big hands and he used to ruffle my hair all the time.'

'He liked a pint…but I never saw him drunk.'

'He could stop me misbehaving… He would make me laugh.'

He described Mr K's best feature as 'everything', and he could not think of anything which he disliked about him.

John returned to visit Mr K when he was about eighteen. However, Mr K had 'gone all empty inside', and did not seem to want him around.

John reported that from the age of eleven he was 'pushed from pillar to post' and often he was moved at a minute's notice, without even being told where he was going.

He enjoyed it when he was placed in secure accommodation because he knew that he was going to remain in the same place for a specific period of time.

John has the following perception of his childhood:

'I would have been okay if people had treated me differently.'

'I was entitled to a family and nobody found me one.'

'My childhood was awful…nobody looked after me properly.'

'I should have had a normal childhood.'

'The staff in the children's homes were only in it for the money.'

John feels that he was sad for the majority of his childhood because of what people did to him.

He acknowledged that he was happy sometimes when he was living with Mr and Mrs K.

John was not able to think of any good things which happened during his childhood and felt that bad things happened to him most of the time.

In looking at things in his childhood that he would like to have changed, John felt that he would have liked to have changed it all. He does not think that he learned anything about being a parent. He learned how to steal cars and not go to school. He reported that the most important lesson he learned was, 'If you don't stick up for yourself, people walk all over you.'

Training exercise/case study

There is a case study which looks at experiences from childhood in the Appendix, Exercise 3.

2.4 EDUCATION

The worker should explore the person's experiences in education and their perception of those experiences. In particular, workers should be looking for the person's understanding of their academic ability and behaviour, how they perceive the value of education and how they think they were perceived by their teachers and the other pupils. Issues of bullying, being bullied and peer relationships are also important.

Use this checklist selectively.

The education checklist

- What schools did you go to?
- What kind of schools were they?
- Did you miss any school?
- Were you ever excluded from school? If so, why?
- Was there a reason why you did not go to school? [if appropriate]
- What kind of pupil do you think you were?
- What were your favourite subjects?
- What were your least favourite subjects?
- Did you leave school with any examination passes?
- Were you in the top streams/groups, middle, or bottom?
- How would your teachers have described you?
- How would your school friends have described you?
- What was the worst thing you did at school?
- What was the thing you were most proud of at school?
- Were you ever bullied at school? If so, by whom and for how long?
- Did you ever bully anyone? If so, whom and for how long?
- Did you have lots of friends or a small group of friends?
- Do you think you could have done better at school?

- What prevented you from doing better at school? [if appropriate]
- Would you like to return to education in the future?

Case study

Michelle's education

Michelle attended Newton Infant and Junior School up to the age of ten.

She was then transferred to Newton Special School, where she completed her education.

Michelle did not like Newton Infant and Junior School, but she was unable to say why. She remembers being bullied and picked on by the other children because they said she smelled.

She enjoyed being at Newton Special School. The lessons were easier and there were fewer children in each class.

Michelle described herself as being 'slow' academically. When this was explored she acknowledged that she has some difficulty with reading and writing.

Michelle described all of her lessons as being ones she enjoyed, but in particular she liked going out on school trips.

She never missed school unless she was ill.

Michelle did not take any examinations.

She thinks her teachers would have described her in the following terms:

'Quiet.'

'Polite.'

'I always did as I was told.'

'Never in trouble.'

The naughtiest thing she did at school was to swear sometimes.

She was most proud of her performance in School Sports Day, describing herself as the best runner in her class.

Even at senior school Michelle was bullied by some of the other children. She remembers telling her mother, who said she should stick up for herself. Eventually she told her teacher and she was not bullied after that.

Michelle did not have a large circle of friends. She did have one special friend and after she left Michelle preferred to stay in class at break time rather than go out and play with the others.

Michelle thinks she did as well as she could at school.

John's education

John calculated that he went to about six schools within the community and also attended education facilities at the secure unit and two of his residential care placements. He described the schools as 'they were special schools but special because I was a troublemaker and not because I was daft'.

John was never really committed to his education and missed school on a regular basis. He acknowledged that he used to be disruptive in class, was often sent to see the headmaster and was excluded from school more times than he can remember. The reasons for his exclusion included fighting, swearing at the teachers, refusing to do as he was told by teachers, and once starting a fire in one of the classrooms.

John would describe himself as a reasonably bright pupil and thinks that if he had tried he would have been able to obtain examination passes. However, at the time when he was due to take examinations, he was serving a sentence in a young offenders institution. In any event he would have refused to take examinations because no-one would have given him a job so there was no point.

John did like some of his subjects, particularly those which required him to use his hands, for example, woodwork and art. He did not like language subjects and considered them to be a waste of time.

John believes that his teachers would describe him in the following terms:

'Disruptive.'

'He would never do as he was told.'

'It was a waste of time trying to teach him.'

'A pain in the backside'.

'He would have done okay if he had applied himself.'

'He was good at art.'

The worst thing that John did at school was to set fire to one of the classrooms. He did this to gain revenge on one of his teachers who had embarrassed him in front of the whole class.

Some of his art work gave John real pride, but he was most proud of his reputation as a troublemaker and disruptive pupil.

John described himself as being the leader of a reasonably large gang of friends who were feared and respected by the other pupils.

John thinks that he could have done better at school if he had applied himself. However, he recognises that the constant change of schooling prevented him from doing better but he also considers that the majority of his teachers were useless and he blames them for the poor quality of his education.

John does not feel that he will ever apply himself to further academic study. He believes that he is a student of life and that is all the education he needs.

Training exercise/case study

There is a case study which looks at education in the Appendix, Exercise 4.

2.5 EMPLOYMENT

Employment records often provide information about achievement and determination. They may identify particular skills. Workers should explore with people significant periods of employment and unemployment to gain an understanding of motivation, job satisfaction and perhaps priorities. The possibility of future employment should be explored.

Use this checklist selectively.

The employment checklist

- What jobs have you had since you left school?
- Why did you change jobs?
- If unemployed, why did you leave your last job?
- If unemployed, when was your last job?
- Which was the job you enjoyed most?
- How many years have you worked?

- How many years have you been available for work?
- If unemployed, would you like to be working?
- If unemployed, what are you doing to obtain employment?
- What is your attitude to work?

Case study

Michelle's employment

Michelle has not worked since leaving school.

John's employment

John has not had any permanent employment in his adult life, although from time to time he has taken on casual work.

He has no ambitions for full-time employment. He believes that the system is designed to keep people like him as a permanent underclass.

Training exercise/case study

There is a case study which looks at employment in the Appendix, Exercise 5.

2.6 PERCEPTION OF SELF

This session should be completed with no third parties present, unless there are specific reasons why someone else needs to be there.

This section is divided into two parts. In the first, the person is encouraged to describe themselves in a free narrative way, with the worker providing global areas for comment. The second part requires the worker to focus on specific aspects and therefore ask more specific questions.

Part One involves questions which invite the person to talk about themselves. However, allow the person time to think and express themselves in their own words. This initial response is likely to be the person's perception of themselves. Therefore, if they make exclusively negative comments, that is likely to reflect current feelings about themselves and may indicate an accurate self-perception. The worker should be patient.

The worker should ask for clarification and examples to give full understanding of comments made.

In Part Two the questions seek to understand the person's perception of themselves in particular aspects of mood. They follow a repeating pattern.

Alongside the questions is the need for observation. The worker is seeking to establish aspects of behaviour which are significant, either as core aspects of behaviour or ones which present themselves in response to specific situations. The different behaviours likely to be observed are within the range summarised below.

- **Hostile** behaviour is both challenging and confrontational. It is characterised by direct threat, intimidation and physical confrontation. It is extremely difficult and frequently impossible to undertake assessments in cases where this behaviour is prevalent. The hostility may be an integrated part of behaviour, which therefore impacts on every aspect of the person's life. It may be present in response to certain situations or when particular issues are being discussed, and this may be significant. Children who are exposed to behaviour such as this are likely to be fearful, anxious and withdrawn. They may be at risk of physical injury, either as a result of direct action or incidentally during the person's confrontation with someone else. Their emotional well-being is likely to be adversely affected. Children who observe parents behaving in this way may use them as role models for the future and develop similar hostile behaviours. Hostile behaviour risks other people rejecting them, being alienated from or fearful of them, and this creates an understanding of and relationship with the local community and outside world which is distorted, unhelpful to family function and unhelpful to the child.

- **Aggressive** behaviour is not as extreme as hostile, but creates similar difficulties. Some families use aggression as a mechanism to keep workers at arm's length; in others it may be a reaction to fears they have about what might happen. Like hostile behaviour, aggression is also behaviour which can be integrated into all aspects of the person's presentation or it can be situation, or topic, based. The dangers which this behaviour represents for children are the same as with hostile behaviour.

- **Dominant** behaviour is used in order to directly control people and situations. Dominant behaviour may take the form of physical dominance, psychological dominance, or a combination of both. At its extreme this behaviour involves the dominant person living in their world of constructed emotional and physical comfort whilst those around them are fearful, unhappy and powerless. Children subjected to parenting by persons within this range have a poor self-image and low self-esteem. Their emotional well-being is unlikely to be good. Being parented by such role models is not helpful for the development of good parenting strategies.

- **Assertive** behaviour, used appropriately, is characterised by honesty, directness, acceptance and a positive response. People are both responsible and spontaneous. Comments like, 'I'm not perfect, but...', 'I do not agree with that because...', and 'I take responsibility for my life' are typical. Children who experience this type of behaviour learn that they are individuals in their own right with views they feel confident to express. They are likely to grow up feeling emotionally safe and secure.

- **Passive** behaviour is characterised by indecision, helplessness and submission. Comments like 'Whatever you want to do is okay' and 'I'm not important' are typical. Children whose parents' behaviour is within this range are likely to have a low self-esteem and poor self-image. Parents with this behaviour are less likely to be able to protect their children.

- **Submissive** behaviour is characterised by complete concession to the needs and demands of others. People within this range of behaviour are unable to protect themselves or any children for whom they may have responsibility. They are likely to present as overwhelmed, defeated and extremely compliant. Children will be vulnerable to exploitation by others and may develop strategies to become dominant to the person themselves. They are unlikely to experience reasonable levels of parental control. Whilst the other types of behaviour have elements of self-determination, submissive behaviour is almost always by imposition rather than by choice. Submissive behaviour is a 'victim' indicator.

These different types of behaviour are not mutually exclusive, and people will usually operate across several behaviours depending on the circumstances and relationships. For example, a person might be passive as a preferred behaviour but capable of aggressive behaviour if confronted by certain people or situations. Workers should carefully note the full range of behaviour in as many different situations as possible in order to give a fuller understanding of the person.

Workers should also look for the use of defence mechanisms. Whilst defence mechanisms are a legitimate part of managing, they can also indicate areas of concern. For example, parents who blame everyone but themselves for difficulties are likely to be using 'projection' inappropriately.

The following checklists can be used alongside the *Framework for the Assessment of Children and their Families* (DoH 2000) and the Family Pack of Questionnaires and Scales, including the Adult Well-being Scale which is included in the *Framework*.

Use this checklist selectively.

Checklist for perception of self

- Describe yourself.

- Use words or sentences which you think describe you.

- What do you consider to be the best thing about you?

- What do you consider to be the worst thing about you?

- Describe times when you like to spend time alone.

- When you are alone what do you think about?

- What kind of things make you happy?

- When was the last time you were happy and why?

- Describe the happiest you have ever been in your life.

- How often do you feel happy?

- What do you do when you are happy?

- How long does your happiness last?

- Are you a happier person now than when you were young? If not, why?

- Are you a happier person in the last few years? If not, why?

- What would be needed to make you happy?

- What makes you angry?

- When was the last time you were angry?
- Describe the most angry you have ever been in your life and what happened.
- How often do you feel angry?
- How long does your anger last?
- What do you feel like doing when you are angry?
- What do you normally do when you are angry?
- What do you do to try to control your anger?
- How often does that work?
- Would you like to be angry more often or less often?
- How do you think you could achieve that?
- Are you angry more often now than when you were younger? If so, why?
- Are there specific people who make you angry?
- Are there specific situations which make you angry?
- What makes you feel sad?
- When was the last time you were sad?
- Describe the saddest time in your life.
- What do you feel like doing when you are sad?
- How often do you feel sad?
- How long does your sadness last?
- What do you normally do when you are sad?
- Do you try to do anything to stop feeling sad?
- How often does that work?
- Would you like to be sad less often?
- How do you think you could achieve that?
- Are you sad more often now than when you were younger? If so, why?
- Tell me about specific people who make you feel sad.
- Tell me about specific situations which make you feel sad.

Explore other emotions which are appropriate to the particular person, for example:

- helplessness
- despair
- stress
- despondency
- feeling down
- anxiety
- any others.

Exploring the person's perception of their relationship/interaction with others:

- How would other people describe you?
- How many close friends do you have?
- How easily do you make friends?
- Who is your closest friend?
- Why do you think you are so close?
- How do you get on?
- What do your neighbours think of you?

Exploring the future:

- What would you like to be doing in one year?
- What would you like to be doing in three/five/ten years?
- What changes, if any, do you think you will make in the future?

Exploring overall perceptions:

- In your whole life, what percentage have you been:
  - happy
  - sad
  - a bit of both/in between

- At present, how much of the time are you:
  - happy
  - sad
  - a bit of both/in between.
- Would you like to change that?
- What would be needed to change that?

Case study

Michelle's perception of herself

Michelle described herself in the following terms:

'I like to be quiet.'

'I am not one for crowds.'

'I am not very good at some things.'

'I don't like being on my own.'

'I would do anything for anyone.'

'People say I don't have much confidence.'

Michelle considers that her best feature is her 'quietness' and the thing she likes least about herself is 'that I am too fat'. She was unable to think of anything about her personality which she did not like.

She likes to be quiet, but not alone, and sometimes feels afraid when she is in the house by herself.

She is happy when:

'John is in a good mood.'

'When John is being nice to her.'

'John is happy.'

'When there are not a lot of people around.'

'When she is watching her favourite TV programmes.'

'When she sees David.'

The last time Michelle was happy was when she saw David. He makes her laugh and she likes that.

The happiest she has ever been in her life was when she used to spend time with her grandmother, but that was a long time ago.

Michelle reported that she does not feel that happy very often at present as there are a lot of arguments, and because John is angry with her about David being taken away from them. John says that it is her fault David is in care.

Michelle does not do anything in particular when she is happy, although she does like the feeling and she likes it to last as long as possible.

Michelle sees herself as a less happy person than she was before. She feels less happy, less often, since her grandmother died.

Michelle does not see herself as being an angry person. She thinks the last time she was angry was when David was taken away by the social workers.

She was unable to recollect when she had been most angry in her life. She feels anger very infrequently and she does not think that her angry periods last for very long.

If Michelle does become angry she quickly becomes upset and tends to cry. She was unable to explain ways in which she would try to control her anger. She believes that she would like not to be angry at all. She was unable to think of any ways in which she might achieve this.

Michelle thinks it is possible that she is angry more often now than when she was small. She does get angry at social workers sometimes because she believes they have tried to ruin her life. She feels angry sometimes when she is having contact with David and he does not want to play with her.

Michelle feels sad that David has been taken away from her because she can only see him on three occasions each week. She also feels sad because John shouts at her sometimes and because she has fallen out with her mother and father.

The saddest time in her life was when her grandmother died. Michelle reported that she still cries when she thinks about this.

When she is sad, Michelle usually cries, and after she has had a good cry the sadness seems to go away a little bit.

Michelle would never like to be sad again because it upsets her, but she was unable to think of ways in which she would be able to achieve this.

She does not remember feeling particularly sad when she was younger, and thinks she is becoming a more sad person as she gets older.

John says nasty things to her sometimes, which makes her feel sad, and she feels sad when the contact sessions with David end.

Michelle thinks that people would describe her in the following terms:

'Stupid.'

'Quiet…shy.'

'She does not like going out much.'

'She isn't very good at anything.'

Michelle does not have any friends, although John's friends come to visit them at home. She has never had any friends since she left school because of her shyness, and feels embarrassed and nervous if she is somewhere where there are a lot of strangers.

Michelle thinks that her closest friend is John. She thinks they are so close because they live together and they talk to each other sometimes.

Michelle tends to keep herself to herself and so she does not know many people who live close by. She thinks they probably know her because she has lived in Newton all of her life.

Michelle likes to get up at the same time each day and to know what she is going to be doing for the rest of the day. She prefers to have her meals at set times of the day and plans things around activities such as meal times, visiting David and television programmes. If her daily routine is disrupted she feels that she becomes unsettled and finds it difficult to fit everything in. Sometimes she can become angry with people if they mess up her day, but she does not say anything.

Michelle found it impossible to conceptualise what she would be doing in the future. She does want to stay with John and she wants to be able to look after David. She does not want to make any changes and she wants things to be as they were before David was taken into care.

In looking at her whole life, Michelle felt that she had been happy for most of the time and sad for a little bit of the time.

In exploring how she sees her life now, she believes that she is sad more often than she is happy. She would like to change that to being happy for most of the time, but was unable to say how she would achieve this.

John's perception of himself

John described himself in the following terms:

'I look after myself…nobody gets one over on me.'

'I can be okay with people, if they are okay with me.'

'People know not to wind me up.'

'Once I have made my mind up about something that's it.'

'Once I have made my mind up about someone that's it.'

'I like a good laugh.'

John thinks that the best thing about him is that 'I can look after myself,' and the worst thing about him is that 'I sometimes don't see people taking advantage of me until it's too late.'

John does not see himself as a happy person. He tends to be happy when he is on drugs because he is able to forget the mess that people have made of his life. The happiest he has ever been was when his daughter Aimee was born, although that happiness was taken away from him because social workers interfered and she had to go and live with Dianne's parents.

He generally only feels happy when he is under the influence of drugs and his happiness lasts until he is coming down.

He does not see himself as being as happy now as when he was young, and he has not been particularly happy in recent years.

He would feel happier if people would stop interfering in his life.

The following things make John angry:

'People interfering in my life.'

'People telling me what to do.'

'People messing me about.'

'People saying that I have injured David.'

'People who tell me lies.'

'Michelle when she winds me up.'

'People who hurt kids.'

John feels angry most of the time at the moment.

The most angry he has ever been was when he was eleven years old and he was told that his foster carer Mrs K had died.

His anger lasts for as long as people continue to wind him up or upset him. John does not accept that he becomes angry with himself or as a result of his own actions. He believes that he becomes angry because of the actions of other people.

He feels that he is 'capable of anything', when he is really angry and that sometimes 'the red haze comes down and I don't remember anything afterwards'.

When he is angry he will do whatever is needed to sort the problem out. If that means resorting to physical violence, John feels it is justified.

John does not feel that he needs to control his anger. He feels that if people stop winding him up he does not become angry.

The following things are likely to make John feel sad:

'Seeing children suffer.'

'Not being able to see Aimee' [his daughter].

John does not see himself as a sad person, considering that sadness is a waste of time and energy.

The saddest time in his life was when Mrs K died. He remembers crying a lot then. When this was further explored, John reported that this was the last time that he cried. He made a decision then that he would never cry again. He now sees crying as a sign of weakness.

John feels that people would perceive him in exactly the same terms as he perceives himself.

He has a small circle of friends but none he would describe as close to him. John explained that, 'If you let people get too close to you, they will either take advantage of you or let you down.'

He keeps himself to himself and expects other people to do the same. He does not know what people in the neighbourhood think of him, nor does he care. He thinks they are probably afraid of him. He expects them to keep themselves out of his business.

John feels that he is in control of his life, and he is the one who makes the decisions about what he will or will not do.

He does not know what he will be doing in one year's time or at any time in the future, nor does he care. He explained that he lives one day at a time and that's how everyone should be.

In looking at his whole life, John feels that he has been sad for the majority of the time. At the present time, because he refuses to let sadness prevail, he is neutral for the majority of the time. He thinks he would be happier if people would 'get off my case'.

Training exercise/case study

There is a case study which looks at perception of self in the Appendix, Exercise 6.

2.7 IDEAL SELF

It is helpful to explore the person's ideal self. People would usually want to change something about themselves, for example, be more assertive or lose their temper less often. Someone who is satisfied with themselves might be content with what they have achieved, and this is positive. However, it may be that s/he has areas of dysfunction that s/he does not recognise, and being content with themselves might indicate a reluctance to change or an inability to change.

S/he might be dysfunctional but not aware of the impact of this on her/himself.

Someone who recognises that they could be a better person is more likely to be motivated to change, and capable of such change.

There is discretion in the use of this checklist.

Checklist for ideal self

- Are you happy with the person you are?
- Tell me about any changes you would like to make to yourself.
- Do you think those changes would make you a happier person?
- Do you think those changes will help you with your relationships?
- Do you think the changes would make you a better person?
- Do you think these changes would help you to look after the children in a better way?
- If you could be like someone else who would that be?

2.8 SELF-ESTEEM

People who have a good level of self-esteem tend to have lots of confidence in themselves and their ability to do things. They generally consider themselves to be people of worth who are useful and valuable. They believe they are well liked by others and they like themselves. A good self-esteem is a positive indicator for the care of children.

People with a poor self-esteem have a low opinion of themselves. They believe themselves to be failures, unattractive and useless. Emotional energy is usually low and they find child care responsibilities more difficult.

People with a good level of self-esteem are more likely to be able to tackle change and more able to accommodate change.

The checklist looks at different areas which have an impact on self-esteem, so that an overview about the person's self-esteem can be formed. In addition, specific aspects within that can be identified. For example, having completed the checklist, workers can revisit particular questions and further explore the person's thinking. The question about 'family members making the person feel they are not good enough' may establish that this is something which significantly affects the person's self-esteem. This may be worthy of note in the evaluation and may help in other aspects of the assessment, for example when looking at support systems from within the family.

This checklist should be applied in its entirety.

○ indicates good self-esteem

□ indicates poor self-esteem

△ is a neutral indicator, except that a number of these represent a possible lack of co-operation or an inability on the part of the person to understand themselves.

Checklist for self-esteem

	Yes	No	Don't Know
Do you feel you can do things as well as most other people?	O	□	△
Are there things you are proud of?	O	□	△
Do you often think you are a failure?	□	O	△
Do you feel you are not as good as other people?	□	O	△
In general are you pretty sure of yourself?	O	□	△
Do you often wish you were someone else?	□	O	△
Would you find it very difficult to make a speech?	□	O	△
Are there a lot of things about you that you would change if you could?	□	O	△
Do you think you are quite popular with people in general?	O	□	△
Do you have a great deal of confidence in your decisions?	O	□	△
Do you have a good opinion of yourself?	O	□	△
Do you often feel ashamed of things you have done?	□	O	△
Do you feel photographs do not do you justice?	□	O	△
Do you think there are family members who make you feel you are not good enough?	□	O	△
Do you get upset if someone criticises you?	□	O	△
Do you think other people regard you as being useless?	□	O	△
Do you sometimes question your worth/value as a person?	□	O	△

When people say nice things about you do you find it difficult to believe/accept?	□	○	△
Do you sometimes remain silent because you feel people will laugh at what you say?	□	○	△
Are you shy in social situations?	□	○	△
Do you feel you are as good as other people?	○	□	△
Do you feel you can succeed in doing things you want to?	○	□	△
Are you happy with the way you look?	○	□	△
Are you often shy with other people because you think you will be rejected?	□	○	△
Do you find it difficult to do things in a way which other people think is good?	□	○	△
Do you often pretend to be better at things than you really are?	□	○	△
Do you sometimes feel you can never do anything right?	□	○	△
Do you think you are physically attractive?	○	□	△
Do you feel you have a normal amount of respect for yourself?	○	□	△
Do you think your personality is attractive?	○	□	△

A person with self-esteem would generally score two-thirds of the questions in the good self-esteem range. It may be helpful to score two points for a good self-esteem indicator, no points for a poor self-esteem indicator and one point for a 'do not know'. Therefore forty points is the line above which good self-esteem is likely to be achieved. It is important, however, to compare the checklist results with observations and to test the answers given by the person against the worker's own professional view of them. If necessary the worker should score the checklist themselves and compare the result with the person's responses.

Training exercise/case study

There is a case study which looks at self-esteem in the Appendix, Exercise 7.

2.9 EXPLORING WHETHER PEOPLE ARE ORGANISED OR DISORGANISED, RIGID OR FLEXIBLE

Exploring whether a person is organised or disorganised, flexible or rigid is important because flexible parents are more likely to find ways of responding that are appropriate to the needs of the children. They are less likely to be upset by sudden changes in routine and generally have better coping strategies. Rigid parents are more likely to have a set of responses which they have learned and which they apply in the same or similar situations. The situation has to fit the response rather than the other way round, and this might not always serve the best interests of the children. When children upset routines or systems, rigid parents are more likely to become angry. They are more easily stressed by sudden changes or impositions and their coping mechanisms come under pressure.

Most parents are likely to have combinations of flexibility and rigidity in their behaviour and thinking. Good parenting involves the appropriate use of parental authority and therefore parents should be prepared to be firm/rigid over issues where they feel parental control is necessary. Apart from that, however, they should generally be responsive, reactive and flexible. Parents with the ability to accommodate, compromise and negotiate provide a healthier emotional climate for their children.

People who are entirely flexible are likely to have no organisation in their systems and routines. This can lead to a chaotic lifestyle and the absence of appropriate child care arrangements.

People who are flexible are more likely to be prepared and able to adapt their behaviour and to accommodate different ways of behaving and responding. Rigid people are less likely and less prepared to make changes.

A person's ability to be flexible or rigid should be considered within the context of both their thinking and behaviour.

Organised parents have better systems for the care of children. They become less flustered and can cope with the demands children make on them. Disorganised parents are more likely to develop a child care regime which is more inclined towards being chaotic. 'Organised' should not mean 'regimented' because that inhibits the child's development and is more likely to be designed for the comfort of the parent.

Child care and family systems should have an order and therefore be underpinned by being organised. Good parenting has a flexibility which overlays that, allowing for an appropriate response to the unexpected and allowing the child some autonomy.

The checklist of questions which follows should be evaluated throughout the assessment alongside observations which seek to identify behaviour, and also comments, that indicate levels of flexibility and rigidity, organised and disorganised thinking and behaviour.

This checklist is of most value if all the questions are asked.

Checklist for rigid and flexible, organised or disorganised thinking and behaviour

- Are you an organised or disorganised person?
- How do you feel if you do not know what is going to happen from day to day?
- If things are not planned, how do you feel?
- If something suddenly crops up which you had not expected, how do you feel?
- Do you like to follow the same routines?
- How do you feel if you do not know what is going to happen next?
- Do you have a daily routine which you prefer to follow?
- What do you do if your routine is disrupted?
- How do you feel if your routine is disrupted?
- If you are going somewhere, do you always give yourself plenty of time in case something goes wrong?
- How do you feel if something you have planned gets disrupted?
- What do you do if something you have planned gets disrupted?
- If you have already made up your mind about something, do you tend not to change it?
- Do you like the children to have the same routine every day?
- What do you do if the children do not want to follow that routine?

- Does your partner feel the same as you about these things? If not, how does that make you feel?

- Has there ever been a time when things were different and you felt better able to cope?

Case study

Michelle's flexible/rigid, organised/disorganised thinking and behaviour

Michelle prefers to be organised, although she always feels disorganised and this upsets her.

She likes to have a set routine each day. She always gets up at the same time and does things in a set manner. When things occur which she has not anticipated, she feels anxious/worried and sometimes she feels she cannot cope. There have been times when she has become angry at sudden changes but mostly she tends to cry.

Michelle finds it difficult because David upsets her routines all the time. He never goes to bed when she wants him to.

Michelle does have ideas and views, but she finds it very difficult to stick with them when someone else wants to do something different or they disagree with her.

Things were different when she lived with her grandmother. They had a set routine each day and they did the same things each week. She preferred it like that.

John's flexible/rigid, organised/disorganised thinking and behaviour

John does not see himself as organised in any way. He resents organisation because it controls what he does. He comes and goes as he pleases and does what he wants when he wants.

Changes do not bother him. He sees changes and surprises as a challenge.

He hates it when he knows what will happen tomorrow and the next day because that is boring and predictable. He hates prison because of that very fact.

However, once he has decided to do something, then nothing and no-one will stop him.

When John has made his mind up about something he will not change it for anyone. Even if he feels the other person has a good point, he will not change.

Training exercise/case study

There is a case study which looks at rigid/flexible and organised/disorganised thinking and behaviour in the Appendix, Exercise 8.

2.10 EXPLORING DOMINANT AND SUBMISSIVE BEHAVIOUR

Dominant behaviour usually places the person in a position of power over others. That power can be used to gain control over other people's lives in order to achieve a particular state of affairs, for example create a lifestyle in which the dominant person has everything done for them. Alternatively, it can be used so that the person feels powerful. The victims of dominant behaviour are likely to have their actions restricted and their feelings, opinions and wishes ignored. They are likely to feel fearful, inhibited, anxious and unhappy. Their emotional well-being will be adversely affected. When dominant behaviour is associated with power and control, partners can suffer physical and emotional torment and children are at risk of significant harm.

Submissive behaviour usually leaves the person vulnerable to exploitation from others. Their self-esteem is low and they have a poor self-image. Submissive people have difficulty in exercising parental authority or protecting themselves or their children from the actions of others, including exploitation by others.

This checklist is of more value if all the questions are asked, as it gives a more complete picture of dominant and submissive aspects of behaviour.

Checklist for dominant and submissive behaviour

- Do you think you are a very confident person?
- Do you like to do things your way?
- Do you stand up for yourself if you think you are in the right?
- Will you argue with people if you think you are in the right?
- Do you argue with people even if you know you are wrong?
- What kind of things do you argue about?
- If you are in the wrong would you admit it?
- If you have done something wrong would you apologise?
- Do you usually end up being in charge of things?
- What do you do if people try to take over?
- Do you consider yourself to be a nervous person?
- Do you find making decisions difficult or easy?
- Does anyone else make important decisions for you?
- Do you think showing emotions is a sign of weakness?
- Do you insist that people apologise to you if they are in the wrong?
- Do you sometimes become angry with people to make your point?
- Do you sometimes pretend to be angry to get your own way?
- Do you think crying is a sign of weakness?

Case study

Michelle's tendency to dominant or submissive behaviour

Michelle does not feel confident very often.

She finds she very rarely does things her way and seems to spend most of her time doing them in ways which suit others.

She has tried standing up for herself in the past but generally she feels that 'people walk all over me'.

She has never been one to argue with others. She feels she is rarely right.

She prefers not to be responsible for things and does not feel she would like to be in charge of anything.

She apologises if people say she is in the wrong.

When she has done something wrong she feels able to say sorry.

Michelle has been told she is a nervous person and she agrees with that.

She does not find making decisions easy and sometimes worries when she knows a decision has to be made. She prefers John to make the decisions and he seems to enjoy that.

She is an emotional person, she gets upset and cries quite a lot and John has told her she is weak.

Michelle does think it is important for people to apologise if they have done something wrong but she finds that people rarely do.

She does not become angry to make her point and she does not think she has ever pretended to be angry with anyone.

John's tendency to dominant or submissive behaviour

John considers himself to be a confident person.

He likes things to be done his way and he usually insists that is what happens.

He always stands up for himself if he thinks he is in the right, and he will argue with people. Even if he realises he is in the wrong he will still argue, because 'otherwise people just walk all over you'.

He always feels he is in charge of things. He does not let people take over as he does not trust them. If people try to take over he gets angry with them.

John makes all of his own decisions because people have ruled his life too much in the past.

He believes that crying and showing emotions are bad because 'people think you are a soft touch and try to take advantage of you'.

He never has to pretend to be angry. Anger is something he feels a lot of the time.

Training exercise/case study

There is a case study which looks at dominant and submissive behaviour in the Appendix, Exercise 9.

2.11 ALCOHOL ABUSE

Workers should never underestimate the impact of alcohol, drug and substance abuse on the capacity to care for children. Parents who abuse alcohol are likely to become entirely preoccupied with their dependency. Friendships develop within the alcohol dependency subculture and friends outside of that group either are alienated or choose to become disengaged. Family relationships can become strained as standards of child care and personal circumstances deteriorate. Isolation from support systems usually results. Priorities change – for example, the purchase of alcohol becomes more important than the purchase of food. The children's physical and emotional needs are less important than the adult's needs for alcohol. Child care is neglected. Alcohol is expensive and this impacts on the amount of money available for other things. Debts and non-payments become an issue, rent arrears and the disconnection of essential services become real problems. The first signals are often a deterioration in clothing, children presenting as unkempt and arriving at school late or not at all. They are frequently hungry and may even scavenge for food. The absence of intervention at this stage can result in children becoming self-reliant and self-responsible, signs that no-one is exercising parental responsibility.

Never underestimate how difficult it is to stop drinking. Not only is there a physical dependency to overcome, but the underlying emotional/ psychological reasons need to be addressed. People do sometimes give up alcohol of their own initiative and determination, but that is the exception rather than the rule and expert help is usually needed.

People who are undertaking detoxification or withdrawal programmes are likely to present behaviours which are not typical, and account should be taken of this within the assessment. Sometimes the contamination to behaviour, attitudes and belief systems is so significant that an accurate assessment is impossible.

It is important to stress to the person that an honest report is necessary, so that a full and accurate understanding can be gained. Child protection plans made on the basis of inaccurate information are less likely to be successful and that serves the best interests of neither the children nor the adults involved. Workers should always be alert to under-reporting, as people find it difficult to admit to the extent of their alcohol use. Experience shows that most people will not admit to the exact amount they drink. Wherever possible, reliable independent sources of information should be used to assist in exploring levels of use.

There is discretion in the use of this checklist.

Checklist for alcohol abuse

- When did you first begin to drink?
- Why did you start drinking at this time?
- What amount were you drinking?
- Describe your alcohol history since you started.
- How much are you drinking at present?
- What is your present pattern of drinking?
- Do you drink at home, drink out, or both?
- Do you drink alone?
- If not, who do you drink with and why do you drink with them?
- How often do you drink?
- Do you sometimes drink until you pass out?
- What is the effect of alcohol on your behaviour?
- How much a week do you spend on alcohol?
- Where does the money come from?
- How often have you sold furniture, clothing or personal items to buy drink?
- Why do you think you use alcohol?
- Do you consider yourself to have a serious alcohol abuse problem? Are you an alcoholic?
- How often do you associate mainly with other people who drink?
- How often do you think you have not looked after yourself properly when you have been drinking?

- Have you ever suffered from physical or mental health difficulties as a result of your drinking?
- How often have you not taken care of the child(ren) properly when you have been drinking?
- How often have you been drinking whilst you have had the care of the child(ren)?
- How often have you been drunk whilst looking after the child(ren)?
- Have you ever received professional help to give up alcohol? If so, what happened?
- Have you ever tried to give up alcohol without professional help? If so, what happened?
- What normally happens to the child(ren) when you are drinking?
- Would you like to give up alcohol?
- How do you think you could do that?
- What do you think your partner feels about your drinking?
- What do you think your child(ren) feel about your drinking?

Case study

Michelle and issues of alcohol

Michelle was introduced to alcohol by John.

She does not drink now because John says it costs too much for them both to drink.

John and issues of alcohol

John first started to drink as a youngster. Everyone in the Children's Home was stealing cider from a local off-licence and John joined in. He liked being able to forget and found that he did not feel as ill after drinking alcohol as he did after glue-sniffing.

He has used alcohol on a regular basis since then and has frequently used it with drugs. He tends to use it as often as he can afford it and most of the time he drinks with his group of drug-using friends. He prefers to drink strong cider as it gets him drunk more quickly.

He reported that he never passes out because of the drugs or alcohol.

John refused to say how much alcohol costs him each week or where he gets the money.

He does not consider that he is an alcoholic, taking the view that he could give it up if he wanted.

He feels that he would be able to look after children if he was drinking. He did acknowledge that one of the reasons his daughter Aimee was placed with her maternal grandparents was because he was drinking heavily at that time. However, he says he does not drink to that extent now. He does not see the need to stop drinking if he is looking after children. He stated that he can hold his drink and is never drunk.

John does not intend to stop drinking, nor has he ever considered seeking help to do so. He says everybody he knows drinks and they are allowed to keep their children at home.

He does not care what Michelle or David think about his drinking.

Training exercise/case study

There is a case study which looks at alcohol abuse in the Appendix, Exercise 10.

2.12 DRUG ABUSE

The same issues which are pertinent to the abuse of alcohol are also present with the abuse of drugs. However, additional issues need to be raised and these are listed in the checklist below.

Drug abuse is an expensive habit. The issue of cost and where the money comes from should be carefully explored. Theft, shoplifting, borrowing and prostitution often feature as income sources. The risk of prison sentence becomes an issue.

Different drugs have a significantly different effect on people, and this should be explored in detail.

There is discretion in the use of this checklist.

Checklist for drug abuse

- When did you start taking drugs and what is your drug history?
- How many drugs are you presently using?
- How much do you spend on drugs?
- How often does your drug use also involve alcohol?
- What are your preferred drugs?
- How often do you mix drugs together?
- Do you use prescription drugs, such as sleeping tablets, as well?
- Do you have a reliable drug source?
- How do you take the drugs?
- How do the drugs affect you?
- How do you get your needles?
- How do you make sure your gear is clean and safe?
- What do you do with your used needles?
- Where do you keep your drugs and equipment?
- Is there any way the children could gain access to these?
- Did you continue to use drugs during pregnancy? [if applicable]
- What is the effect of drugs on the foetus?
- What efforts did you make to give up when pregnant? [if applicable]
- How often have you taken drugs in front of the child(ren)?
- What do the child(ren) know about your drug habit?
- How often have you taken drugs when you have been looking after the child(ren)?
- What does/do the child(ren) know about the different ways of taking drugs?
- How often do people come to your home to take drugs?
- What detoxification programmes have you tried?

- Which Drug Project are you registered with?
- How long do you consider you have been a drug addict?
- Would you like to stop taking drugs?
- To what extent do you think taking drugs affects your ability to look after a child?
- How often would you look after the child(ren) when you were taking drugs?
- What do you think your partner feels about you taking drugs?
- What do you think the child(ren) feel about you taking drugs?
- What do you think of your partner's use of drugs?
- Have you discussed your views with your partner? If so, what happened?
- How do you feel when your partner is taking drugs?

Case study

Michelle on the issue of drugs

Michelle has never taken drugs of any kind.

She is aware that John uses 'a lot' but is not sure exactly how much.

She feels they are sometimes short of money because John buys his drugs before anything else. At the beginning of their relationship she spoke to him about this but he hit her and she has not asked him again.

Michelle usually tried to keep out of the way with David when John and his friends were in the flat using drugs, because they always made a lot of noise and she felt frightened. However, he would sometimes make David and her stay in the lounge and she would have to make food and drinks for them.

Michelle would like John to stop taking drugs but she knows that he will not.

John on the issue of drugs

John started sniffing glue when he was about twelve years of age and this continued throughout most of his teenage years.

He started smoking cannabis when he was about eighteen years of age and continues to smoke that on a regular basis.

In his early twenties he injected amphetamine sulphate for several years and had a serious addiction. This drug kept him awake for long periods and made him feel good. He stopped taking it when it was no longer having the desired effect.

It was also in his early twenties that John started using heroin. He quickly started to inject the heroin and this has been his drug of choice in recent years.

There was a period when he was in prison when he was taking no drugs at all, and for a while when he first moved to Newton he was only using drugs occasionally.

However, he got in with a group of friends who were using and started using temazepam and methadone, which he bought on the streets. He returned to heroin approximately three years ago.

John reported that he uses as much heroin as he can afford. He refused to say how much that is. He has a regular source which he considers to be reliable.

He tends to acquire his needles from friends, but insists that he does not share needles and usually keeps his gear with him wherever he goes.

John does not think that children are adversely affected if they see adults taking drugs. Dianne and himself regularly used to inject themselves when the children were present.

From time to time friends visit John's flat and he does not object if they want to take drugs. He did not think this bothered David.

John has never been on any specific drug detoxification programmes. He came off whilst he was in prison and feels that if he really wants to stop taking drugs he can manage that for himself. However, he enjoys taking drugs and intends to continue to do so in the foreseeable future. If at some time in the future he decides to stop, that will be his decision, he will not be influenced by anyone else.

John feels that even when he is taking drugs he is a competent and capable parent. He does not believe that drugs have any effect on his alertness, or diligence in matters of safety. He never passes out after injecting. If David came back to live with Michelle and himself he would continue to take drugs.

John does not care what Michelle thinks about his drug-taking. He considers it to be none of her business.

Training exercise/case study

There is a case study which looks at drug misuse in the Appendix, Exercise 11.

2.13 ANGER AND VIOLENCE

Anger and violence have a significant impact on personal function, interpersonal relationships and social interactions. Anger leads to verbal abuse and physical violence. In some cases it leads to self-harm. Children who are victims of anger and violence risk being physically hurt and having their emotional well-being adversely affected. Adults who are victims of violence frequently find themselves locked into relationships from which they desperately want to disengage, but fear, isolation and poor alternatives prevent them from taking positive action. Adults who temporarily flee violent relationships, only to return, do so sometimes out of profound fear, or because they feel that they have no other choices. Some victims accept that violence is a price they are prepared to pay for perceived benefits – for instance, companionship or assistance with child care. They frequently do not see, or are unable to accept, the consequences of this for the emotional and physical well-being of the children. Their ability to protect their children from the effects of anger and violence is greatly diminished.

Perpetrators of violence, people who become angry and people who place no internal controls on their anger place those around them at risk of significant harm. Their behaviour, in part or in total, must be viewed as a negative indicator in terms of their ability to provide for the safe care of children.

Anger is considered within the checklist for perception of self (pp.73–76). However, if anger is a significant feature, more detailed examination may be necessary. This section does not ask whether anger is a feature, it presumes that anger is known to be a feature, and the issues are addressed on that basis.

The following checklist on aggressive tendencies is designed to gain an understanding of the level of aggression the person has, and to understand their responses in certain situations.

The next checklist, on anger/violence within the adult relationship, is in two parts, the first for the perpetrator of violence, and the second for the victim of violence.

The final checklist looks at acceptance of responsibility for violent behaviour.

The checklists are of most value if all of the questions are asked.

Checklist on aggressive tendencies

- If someone did something against you, would you do something to get revenge?
- Would you let them know you were after them?
- What sort of thing would you do if you were very angry?
- Have you ever thought of hurting yourself when you have been really angry?
- What would you do if someone insulted you?
- Has there ever been a time when you really wanted to hurt someone?
- Do you enjoy watching violent films?
- How do you feel when you see blood?
- How often do you get angry enough to yell and swear at people?
- When was the last time and what happened?
- If people let you down how quickly do you forgive them?
- Did you get involved in fights when you were growing up?
- Would you hit someone if they were being verbally abusive to you?
- Do you think people who refuse to fight are cowards?
- Do you think you are angry more often than most people?
- How many times have you smashed things in the house when you have lost your temper?
- When was the last time and what happened?
- What is the most violent thing you have ever done?

- Could you imagine doing anything like that again?
- What would you do if someone was prodding you in the chest to make a point?
- If someone upsets you would you get angry with them?
- Do you get angry with people who get on your nerves?
- What would you do if someone was making fun of you?
- What would you do to someone who was showing off?
- Have you any convictions for violence?
- Have you ever been arrested for violence?
- Do you consider yourself to be an aggressive person?
- Do you consider yourself to be a violent person?
- Do you think other people see you as an aggressive or violent person?
- Do other people think you are someone who can look after yourself in an argument or fight?

Checklist for anger/violence within the adult relationship – pepertrator

- When you lose your temper do you say things to make your partner feel small?
- Do you sometimes demand to be answered when you have asked something?
- Do you say things which you know will hurt and upset your partner?
- Have you ever physically chased your partner in anger?
- Have you ever grabbed your partner in anger?
- Have you ever hit or threatened to hit your partner?
- Have you ever kicked or threatened to kick your partner?
- Have you ever thrown anything at your partner?

- Have you ever attacked your partner with a weapon?
- Have you ever attempted to choke or strangle your partner?
- How often would you say incidents of violence happen?
- When was the last time something happened?
- Are the incidents becoming more or less frequent?
- Why do you think you hit your partner?
- Do you feel you have the right to hit your partner?
- How do you think your partner feels about your behaviour?
- Do you think you will continue with this behaviour?
- Would you like to stop this behaviour? If so how do you think this can be achieved?

Checklist for anger/violence within the adult relationship – victim

- When your partner loses their temper do they say things which make you feel small?
- Do they sometimes demand to be answered when they have asked you something?
- Does your partner say things which they know will hurt and upset you?
- Have you ever been chased after by your partner in anger?
- Have you ever been grabbed by your partner in anger?
- Have you ever been hit or threatened with being hit by your partner?
- Have you ever been kicked or threatened with being kicked by your partner?
- Has your partner ever thrown anything at you? If so, what?

- Has your partner ever attacked you with a weapon?

- Has your partner ever tried to choke or strangle you?

- How often would you say these incidents happen?

- When was the last time something happened?

- Are these incidents becoming more or less frequent?

- Why do you think your partner hits you?

- Do you think your partner should hit you?

- Do you think your partner's behaviour will continue?

- Would you like your partner to stop hurting you? If so, how do you think that will be achieved?

Checklist for accepting responsibility for angry/violent behaviour

- Do you only become really angry or violent when you have been drinking or taking drugs?

- Is threatening some people sometimes the only way of getting things done?

- Do you think that once you get violent it is impossible to stop yourself?

- When you have been violent can you remember what you have done?

- Do you become violent because that is what your parents did in similar situations?

- Do some people make you so angry you have to get violent?

- Do you accept that you get violent every now and again because that is the way you are made?

- Do people exaggerate the damage you have done?

- When you become angry/violent, is it sometimes your fault?

Case study

Michelle's responses on the checklist for angry/violent behaviour

Michelle does not see herself as an angry or violent person. She has never hit or picked on anyone since she grew up and she does not think she did so as a child.

People tend to insult and pick on her all the time and Michelle says, 'I try to ignore them but I wish they would not do it.

She has never wanted to hurt anyone because she knows how that feels, she hates the sight of blood and she closes her eyes when there is something violent on the television.

She remembers being angry as a child and sometimes she still becomes angry. However, she thinks that if she lost her temper other people would get angry with her and she would become upset.

People pick on her quite often and she tends to forgive them fairly quickly. If she did not she would not have any friends at all.

Michelle thinks fighting is stupid. People who refuse to fight are sensible.

She thinks she does not become angry as often as most people she knows, and has never smashed things in a temper. She sometimes feels like hurting herself when she is angry, but never other people.

When she was a child she once threw a toy at her brother and hit him on the head, making it bleed, and she has never done anything like that again.

Sometimes she thinks people are showing off or being rude for no reason but she does not say anything to them.

Michelle's responses on the checklist for victims of angry/violent behaviour

Michelle stated that John probably hits her about once a week, the last time being within the past week. That incident occurred because he had run out of drugs and blamed her for not reminding him. It used to be more often but she tries hard now not to upset him. In the past he has hurt her 'a lot', but she feels that he does not mean it.

John used to hit her more than he does now. It is less frequent now because she now knows what to avoid saying and doing. She has also learned when to keep out of his way.

She had to go to the hospital once when her nose was broken.

She thinks that it is usually her fault when she is hit because she has done something to upset John, and sometimes when he hits her he does not know what he is doing because he has had too much to drink or he is on drugs.

He shouts at her a lot, makes fun of her in front of his friends, and says things on purpose to upset her.

Michelle would like the violence to stop but she does not know how this can be achieved. People have told her she should leave him, but she is afraid because he has said he will find her and kill her. She is also afraid that there would be no-one to look after her if she separated from John.

John's responses to the checklist for angry/violent behaviour

John says he is an aggressive and sometimes violent person, but only because of what other people say and do to him. If they left him alone, then things would not happen.

He is able to 'look after himself' and will do anything necessary to sort a problem out. When this was explored with him, John said that if he was in a fight and he got someone on the floor he would make sure they stayed on the floor. He said he would do anything to win a fight.

He feels that people do not mess with him because they know he will get his own back on them. He knows he has a reputation for being violent and he thinks that people look up to him because of this. He reported that a few years ago he waited twelve months before the opportunity arose for him to assault someone he considered had cheated him over a drug purchase.

He believes that people will take advantage if they think you are weak.

He believes that people only show respect if they are afraid of you.

He considers that threats, anger, violence and aggression are all legitimate ways of getting what he wants.

He refused to talk about his most violent act 'because I was not done for it'.

John has three convictions for violence. In each instance he considers that the violence was justified.

John's responses to the checklist for angry/violent behaviour with partner

John accepts that from time to time he hits Michelle.

However, he blames Michelle for these incidents because she does and says stupid things which wind him up. If she did as she was told, he would not hit her.

He reported that he does not really hurt her, he only gives her a thump to keep her in order.

He hit Michelle the previous week, although he was unable to remember why.

He considers that it is okay to hit her and that she does not mind.

He intends to continue behaving in the same way in the future.

John's responses to the checklist for accepting responsibility for angry/violent behaviour

John does not blame drink or drugs for his aggressive behaviour. However, he commented, 'they don't make me lose my temper, but they don't help me keep it either'.

He accepts that once he has lost his temper, 'the red mist descends', and he goes 'wild'. However, he feels that if people did not wind him up or try to cheat him he would not lose his temper.

He does not accept that he is to blame for his violence. Other people wind him up or cheat him.

Training exercise/case study

There are case studies which look at aggressive tendencies, anger and violence in the Appendix, Exercises 12–14.

2.14 SCHEDULE 1 OFFENCES

Schedule 1 offences are those committed by adults against children. The schedule is contained in the Children and Young Persons Act 1933. People who have convictions for Schedule 1 offences pose a serious risk to children. Consider having this section of the assessment completed by a worker skilled and experienced in this area.

In respect of Schedule 1 offences it is likely that details regarding the offences are in existence. Read these carefully before the session with the person and gain a full understanding of the offending behaviour. Where no record exists, for example, if the offence occurred some time ago, workers can be seriously disadvantaged.

It is important that the person is allowed to give a free narrative account of the offending behaviour. In this way the worker will be able to see whether or not the person's account is accurate compared to known information. For example, the person may omit significant issues or understate the seriousness of the offences.

The worker should go through each offence in some detail. If information is known by the worker but not reported by the person, the worker should revisit the matter after the person has provided their version of events.

Some people become agitated/distressed/angry when offending behaviour is discussed. Workers undertaking the assessment are frequently accused of believing something which the person is denying. It is important to stress to the person that there is a conviction, and that an understanding of that is necessary.

It is important to observe body language and manner, as this will assist in understanding the matter.

The issue of acceptance or denial is significant. Denial is a negative indicator for the person being able to care for children safely. It also prevents engagement with services which could help offenders reduce the level of risk which they present to children.

Many people under-report or understate offending behaviour, and workers should be alert to this.

Explore in detail any specific programmes the person has attended in respect of the offending behaviour, and the person's understanding of the benefits of this.

There is discretion in the use of this checklist.

Checklist for Schedule 1 offences

- How old were you at the time of the offence?
- How old was the victim?
- Did you know the victim? If so, how well did you know him/her?
- How often did you come into contact with him/her?

- Explain what happened.
- How long did the abuse last?
- Who else was involved?
- Why did it stop?
- How did people find out about it?
- What happened in court?
- What sentence did you receive?
- What sentence did anyone else involved receive?
- Do you think the sentence was fair?
- What help did you receive because of the offences?
- Have you attended any courses for people who have committed these type of offences?
- What did you learn from the course?
- Do you know what being a Schedule 1 offender means?
- How do you feel about being a Schedule 1 offender?
- Do you know any other Schedule 1 offenders?
- Have there ever been any circumstances where you have thought about repeating your offending behaviour? If so, what happened?
- Have you ever repeated the offending behaviour and not been found out? If so, what happened?
- Do you think you pose a risk to children?

Training exercise/case study

There are case studies which look at Schedule 1 offences in the Appendix, Exercises 15 and 16.

2.15 CRIMINAL HISTORY

The person's criminal history will sometimes form part of the case papers, and the worker should read this prior to the session. Some offences are significant in terms of child care and child protection. For example if the person is a persistent offender, the risk of a custodial sentence may be real and this will preclude them from a parenting role. Of particular concern are offences of violence and ones which indicate significant involvement in alcohol and drugs.

Offences of violence might include domestic violence, violence within criminal offences, or spontaneous violence in social or interpersonal situations. It is possible to gain a good understanding of the person's violent tendencies and the risk the person poses by exploring these in detail.

Convictions involving drugs and alcohol will provide evidence about lifestyles, possibly some indication of the length of involvement in the abuse and behaviours associated with it, for example, drunk and disorderly. Where convictions involve drug dealing it is possible that the family home has been used as a base. Children are likely to have been exposed to people intoxicated by drugs and to have witnessed violent disputes and disagreements associated with drug dealing. The presence of large quantities of drugs not safely stored poses a risk that children will consume them. The pattern of any offending behaviour and its association with family life can be assessed – for example, where offences are connected with relationship difficulties. Whether or not offending behaviour is current may also be important because of its implications for child care.

The person should initially be allowed to describe their criminal history.

When this has been done the worker should revisit offences which may have a bearing on child care matters or the safe care of children.

An explanation of any offences that the person omitted from their initial account should be obtained.

There is discretion in the use of this checklist.

Checklist for criminal history

- When did you first start to commit criminal offences?
- Why do you think you began to offend?
- What is your criminal history from that time?
- What sentence(s) did you receive?
- Why do you think you committed each offence?
- What was happening in your life at the time of the offence?
- When was your last offence?

- Have you any outstanding court appearances?

- Do you think you will commit offences in the future. If so, why?

- Have you received any counselling or attended any courses in respect of your offending behaviour?

- What did you learn?

- If you are still committing offences, would you like to stop?

- If so, how do you think this will be achieved?

Case study

John's responses to the checklist for criminal offences

1984–1988
Juvenile court appearances for offences of theft and taking without consent, motor vehicles – conditional discharges.

1987
Assault – conditional discharge

1988
Assault occasioning actual bodily harm – young offenders institution, two years.

1991
Possession of drugs with intent to supply – 100 hours community service order.

1991
Breach of community service order – probation order, two years.

1992
Breach of probation order – six months' imprisonment.

1996
Possession of drugs with intent to supply. Grievous bodily harm – two years' imprisonment.

The first violent offence occurred when John was fifteen years of age and, according to John, resulted from a dispute over distribution of the proceeds from a theft. John considered he was not getting his share and gave his partner in crime a thump. At the time of the offence he was on the run from a community home and living around and about with friends.

When he was sixteen years of age and living in a bedsit, John assaulted a girl of eighteen. He knew her vaguely and reported that she made a fool of him in a pub by telling everyone he was under age. He found out where she lived and waited for her one night some weeks afterwards. According to John she got what she deserved, it was her fault, nobody shows him up.

John has two convictions for drug-related offences. At the time of the first he was living rough and doing 'this and that' to make ends meet. The second offence also involved his then partner, Dianne. They were selling drugs from their flat in order to pay for their own habits.

John said of the breaches of the probation and community service orders, 'nobody tells me what to do'. For the same reason, he lost all of his remission in prison.

The final conviction for grievous bodily harm occurred after Dianne had reported him to the police following a domestic disturbance at their flat. After the police left, John 'gave her what she deserved'.

John's view on future offending is that it his business and nothing to do with the assessment. When it was pointed out to John that he could be sent to prison and that this would prevent him from caring for David, he became angry and the session was ended prematurely.

Training exercise/case study

There is a case study which looks at criminal history in the Appendix, Exercise 17.

2.16 HEALTH

Some previous health information may be available and this should be read before this session.

Health can be an important issue. If a person has a persistent health problem, their ability to parent may be impaired. Particular illnesses may be life-threatening; or the person may have a terminal illness. Illness causes stress, and it may be necessary to take this into account. Illnesses such as bulimia and anorexia give clues to a person's emotional health. If conditions are genetic, this too would need to be taken into account. Health care may be an ongoing issue.

The state of the person's health should be recorded, including any serious illnesses or injuries. It is important to understand his/her own perception of their condition, as some may be understated and others exaggerated.

Ask if the person has ever seen a psychiatrist or psychologist, and why. Details should be obtained.

If people are abusing drugs, the risks of HIV/Aids and hepatitis should be explored. This can be a difficult area, as many people who abuse drugs deny these risks and often avoid addressing the health issues. Many avoid or refuse to take the appropriate tests. Drugs and alcohol can lead to serious physical and mental ill-health.

Lifestyles or behaviour exposing people to the possibility of sexually transmitted diseases should also be explored.

There is discretion in the use of this checklist.

Checklist on health

- Describe any serious accidents or illnesses.
- Describe the extent to which you have recovered from them.
- What physical or emotional effect have they had?
- Have you ever been seen by a psychiatrist or psychologist?
- If so, when and why?
- Do you know what they said about you?
- What physical or emotional problems are you being treated for?
- What medications are you currently taking?
- Do you have any illnesses which you believe to be a problem?
- How do you feel about any current illnesses?
- Do any illnesses or injuries affect your ability to look after children?
- Do you require any special help or medical services because of your illness?

> - Do you think your lifestyle exposes you to health risks?
> - What does your partner feel about your illness(es)?

Case study

Michelle's responses to the checklist on health

Apart from the accident which Michelle had when she was eleven years old, she has had no major illnesses or injuries.

John's responses to the checklist on health

John reported that he has had no major illnesses or operations.

He does currently have some problems because the veins in his arms have collapsed and he is injecting into his groin. He has been warned that this is likely to lead to problems with circulation in the future, and to the possibility of amputation of his legs. He has been referred to see a specialist by his doctor, but he does not think that he will attend the appointment.

2.17 PREVIOUS RELATIONSHIPS

The adults' previous relationships, and their involvement in previous child care arrangements, provide significant information about them. The understanding already gained about the individuals' behaviour, perception of themselves and previous life experiences should now be extended to their previous relationships. Information about the pattern of previous relationships can give clues as to how individuals operate, what expectations they have about relationships, and what they expect of themselves in relationships. People are attracted to relationships for different reasons, and this can be explored. The reasons for relationships ending may help to understand whether the person is likely to have long-term relationships or not, and indicate what they are looking for in relationships – for example, they ended a relationship because the partner did not let them go out with friends often enough. People whose relationships end because of domestic violence may have selected indiscriminately, may have a submissive personality which attracts such partners, or may simply have been unlucky. Multiple previous relationships could indicate a clear pattern within relationships which is likely to be repeated, and this enables workers to predict likely future behaviour with more certainty. For example, if someone has been deserted a number of times because their partner has formed a new relationship this is something that would need to be explored in detail. Of particular interest would be the person's understanding of why that pattern has repeated.

The person's subsequent involvement with any children from the relationship, and any parenting experiences gained, can be explored.

There is discretion in the use of this checklist.

Checklist for previous relationships

- Beginning with your first serious relationship, what was the person's name?

- How old were you both?

- What was happening in your life at the time?

- How did you meet?

- What attracted you to each other?

- How long did the relationship last?

- How long did you live together?

- Describe the person.

- What did you like best about him/her?

- What was the worst thing about him/her?

- What were you like together? Describe your relationship.

- How many children did your partner have?

- How many children did you have together?

- Describe how you looked after the children together.

- Why do you think the relationship ended?

- How did you feel about this?

- What happened to the children?
- How do you feel about this?
- Did you have any involvement with social workers? If so, why?
- What do you feel about that relationship now?

Case study

Michelle's previous relationships

Barry J

Michelle met Barry at the Willows Centre. She described the centre as somewhere people go because they need help and support. At the time she was 22 years old and Barry was 30 years old.

Michelle was living at home with her parents and 'helping out around the house'.

She thought Barry was funny because he could pull faces which made her laugh. He was tall and thin and reminded her of the photographs she had seen of her grandfather.

Michelle said they never went out like she does with John sometimes. They never lived together. Their relationship ended after she found out she was pregnant. Her parents 'put a stop to it'.

Michelle explained that she did not mind when the relationship ended as she did not like Barry that much anyway.

She described him in the following terms:

'He was funny sometimes.'

'He got into a mood sometimes.'

'His parents did not like it when I was pregnant.'

She described his nicest feature as, 'He could dance really well,' and she least liked him 'when he was in one of his moods…he would not speak to me'.

Michelle thinks that social workers visited when she was pregnant but stopped when it was decided that she would go and live with her grandmother after the baby was born.

She is glad that they are no longer together because she has got John.

John's previous relationships

Dianne A

John met Dianne when he was twenty-one years old and she was twenty-seven years old. They met through their mutual interest in drugs.

They were together for approximately five years although, according to John, they were probably separated by prison sentences for three of those years owing to Dianne being on remand or serving time for her shoplifting.

John does not know what first attracted him to Dianne and they just ended up living together; he simply moved in. He does not even think he asked Dianne if he could. Just after he moved in, Dianne was remanded for shoplifting, and that was when her children were placed with her parents. John welcomed this, describing them as 'whining little brats'.

He described Dianne in the following terms:

'She was all right sometimes.'

'She did not know when to keep her mouth shut.'

'She knew where to get good gear.'

'She was a useless cook.'

'She wasn't a very good thief, she got caught too often.'

He liked her best when 'she did as she was told', and least when she 'started answering back or arguing with me'.

They did not spend much time together except when they were using drugs. When they were together they argued a lot, but according to John, no more than any other couple. He felt things were better when Dianne was not winding him up.

John thought it was all right when Dianne became pregnant, but he did not think the baby would be born because Dianne was using heavily during the pregnancy. Their daughter Aimee was placed with her maternal grandparents after the social workers said if she remained with them they would apply for an emergency protection order. John remains extremely angry about this. He feels they had no right to do this, he blames Dianne because she was on drugs. He reported that the social workers were satisfied with him.

It was after this that the incident involving the assault on Dianne took place.

John did not see Aimee much after she was placed with her grandparents, and shortly after that he was locked up. He asked for contact when he was inside, but it was refused. When he came out he decided to start a new life. He has not made any efforts to see his daughter. He was unable to describe her in any way. He reported no feelings about this state of affairs.

Training exercise/case study

There is a case study which looks at previous relationships in the Appendix, Exercise 18.

2.18 PRESENT RELATIONSHIP

Information will already have been collected during previous sessions about the relationship between the adults, and the initial views formed, will be a starting-point for exploring current relationship issues. You may want to concentrate on particular areas about which you feel concern, and therefore the checklists may need to be used selectively. The adult relationship impacts upon every aspect of care and sets the emotional climate within the home. Look to see if issues from previous relationships, whether positive or negative, feature in this relationship.

The current relationship is explored here in two separate phases. First of all, a session with each of the adults looks at their concept of each other. That session must be undertaken with the other person absent.

Each partner separately should be given the checklist of relationship statements. Each is a comment about the relationship, and the person has to arrange them in order, beginning with the most important feature of the relationship as number 1, and ending with the least important. Statements which the person considers not relevant can be discarded.

The second session is undertaken with the couple together in order to look at joint issues and explore levels of collaboration and co-operation. When exploring the couple's relationship with them both, it is sometimes helpful to break it down into separate years in order to understand the pattern of the relationship.

Some of the issues are replicated in the course of the single and couple interviews. Different responses within the separate and joint sessions may be indicators of underlying issues within the relationship. For example, one person may indicate in the separate session that they feel left out of decision-making, but agree in the joint session that decisions are taken together.

Issues of particular significance might include:

- how the partners react to each other

- how they interact with each other

- whether the relationship is reciprocal

- issues of dominance within the relationship

- whether either partner is submissive.

There is discretion in the use of the checklists, except for the 'statements about the relationship'. This is the only checklist which would normally be given to the person her/himself to complete. First, check their ability to read, write and comprehend.

Checklist for present relationship

- When did you meet?

- How did you meet?

- How long have you lived together?

- What first attracted you to him/her?

- Describe your partner.

- What do you like most about him/her?

- What do you like least about him/her?

- Do your parents approve of your partner?

- Explain who does what jobs around the house.

- Who makes the important decisions, you or your partner?

- What things do you normally agree about?

- What things do you normally disagree about?

- If you disagree, what normally happens?

- Who pays the bills and normally organises the money?

- What level of respect do you think your partner has for you?

- When you have something to say how well does your partner listen to you?

- Has your partner ever physically hurt you in any way? If so, when and why?

- Does your partner ever say things which hurt or upset you? If so, what and how often?

- If you could change anything about your partner, what would it be?

- If you could change anything about your relationship, what would it be?

- How long do you think you and your partner will stay together?

- Is there anything you can think of which might cause you to separate?

- If you separated, what do you think you would do?

- Are you happy with your relationship?

- If not, what are you unhappy with about your relationship?

- Do you think you will have more children?

- What will your partner think you have said about your relationship?

Case study

Michelle's responses to the checklist on her present relationship

Michelle met John at the fish shop one evening. She was being picked on by some teenagers and was crying and he 'sorted them out. He offered to buy me a drink and I probably had too much. The next thing I remember is waking up the next day, in his flat. I knew my gran would be really upset so I never went back. I said I wanted my baby and John went round but she refused to let us have him. John took him anyway. The police came round later but I told them I wanted to stay with John. We have been together ever since.'

Michelle was twenty-seven years old when they met. She does not know how old John was. She was unable to say what she first found attractive in him.

She described John in the following terms:

'He looks after me.'

'He gets in a bad mood sometimes when he needs a fix.'

'He is tall.'

'People don't mess with him.'

'He sorted my dad out…gave him a thumping when he came to get me.'

'I like him.'

'He shouts at me sometimes.'

Michelle likes 'the way he stops people picking on me' the best, and 'when he gets in a bad mood' is the thing she least likes about him.

Michelle reported that her parents hate John because of the trouble they say he has caused.

Michelle recognises that the flat is not very tidy. This is because she finds it difficult to do some of the jobs. John has told her that it is woman's work and makes her do it all. She is no good at cooking. John does not eat much and she likes to have take-aways, which she gets if John will give her the money.

John looks after the money and pays for everything. He sometimes does things without telling her, but if she does anything then he goes mad with her.

She thinks that John loves her ('he must because he looks after me'), although sometimes, when he really loses his temper, he hits her. This does not happen very often, and when it does Michelle feels it is because she has done or said something wrong. Sometimes he calls her stupid, especially when other people are around, but if anyone else calls her names he goes mad with them. He says she is his property and no-one else picks on her but him.

Michelle stated that John probably hits her once a week, the last time being within the past week. That incident occurred because he had run out of 'stuff' and blamed her for not reminding him. It used to be more often but she tries hard now not to upset him. In the past he has hurt her 'a lot', but she feels that he does not mean it.

She does not feel that John listens to her, but that is because she never has anything useful to say.

Michelle would not want to change anything about her relationship with John. She feels he is perfect. She would like him to stay in sometimes at night, as she becomes frightened by herself, but she feels he is entitled to go out with his mates. She does not go out, as she knows that John would be really angry if she did.

She wants to stay with John forever because he looks after her. She has told him she would like them to have a baby, especially now that David has been taken away, but he has told her they are not having one. Michelle hates needles, but John makes her have an injection at the doctor's to stop her getting pregnant.

She feels they are happy together, she would hate them to separate because there would be no-one to look after her.

Michelle does not know what John would expect her to have said about their relationship.

John's responses to the checklist on his present relationship

John has known Michelle for eight months and they have lived together for the whole of that time.

John would not comment on what first attracted him to Michelle. He did say that she was being exploited at home by her parents. They were taking her benefits and using her for slave labour.

He described Michelle in the following terms:

'She's a good lass, she does as she is told.'

'She doesn't answer back.'

'She never moans when I go out and about.'

'She can't cook.'

'She doesn't use drugs.'

'She's like a little pet dog…quiet.'

'She's got mental problems, sometimes she just sits and cries for nothing.'

He described her best feature as 'she never complains now', and her worst feature as, 'Sometimes she just bursts out crying…for no reason…it makes me angry, that.'

John does not get on at all with Michelle's parents and they have nothing to do with each other.

John explained that Michelle looks after the house, although he has to keep telling her what to do. He makes all the decisions, looks after the money, pays the bills and sees to everything. He feels Michelle is incapable, 'She can't even write her own name properly'.

He expects Michelle to listen to him and do as she is told but he does not listen to her because 'she never has anything useful to say'.

He accepts that he has hit Michelle from time to time because she has been out of order, although it does not happen very often now. She has never tried to hit him back or shown any aggression towards him.

John does not want to change anything about the relationship. He is content with the present arrangements, although he will not say whether they will last in the future. He reports being happy and knows that Michelle is happy.

He does not want children and has told Michelle so.

John states that they will only separate if and when he says so. If they do, he will go somewhere else and do his own thing.

John thinks that Michelle would describe him as 'brilliant'.

Training exercise/case study

There is a case study which looks at the present relationship in the Appendix, Exercise 19.

Statements about your relationship
with your current partner

Number the following list of statements so that the statement about your partner which is most important to you is number 1, and the statement least important to you is number 16.

If any of the statements do not apply to you, cross them out.

I need a man/woman in my life.	
I do not want to start over again with someone else.	
S/he is better than my other partner.	
S/he is a good cook.	
S/he is good with money.	
S/he looks after me.	
S/he makes me feel wanted.	
S/he is a good friend.	
S/he loves me.	
I love him/her.	
I trust him/her.	
S/he is a good parent.	
S/he lets me go out with friends.	
S/he lets me spend money on myself.	
Without him/her I would feel lonely.	
S/he lets me have personal space when I need it.	

Notes on 'relationship with current partner' statements

The following statements indicate an emotional connection between the person and their partner. Based high in the priority list, they are a positive relationship indicator. The lower they are based, the more negative they indicate the relationship is in terms of emotional warmth, love and care:

- S/he loves me.
- I love him/her.
- S/he makes me feel wanted.
- I trust her/him.

The following statements indicate a positive image of the partner, except for 'S/he looks after me', which can also be grouped within the dependency range (based upon what other factors the assessment identifies about the person):

- S/he is a good friend.
- S/he is a good parent.
- S/he is a good cook.
- S/he is good with money.
- S/he looks after me.

The following statements either indicate a level of dependency on the partner, or are generally negative reasons for being in the relationship. Placed high in the list of priorities, these statements indicate a relationship which is not based on emotional warmth, and are a negative indicator for being in the relationship.

- Without him/her I would feel lonely.
- I need a man/woman in my life.
- I do not want to start over again with someone else.
- S/he is better than my other partner(s).

The following statements indicate that a level of autonomy, freedom and personal space is allowed within the relationship. This can be either a positive or negative indicator, depending on other information. For instance, if autonomy is allowed and the relationship is one within which the person dominates his/her partner, then it has negative aspects. However, if autonomy is based upon trust, understanding and a recognition of the need for personal space, it becomes positive:

- S/he lets me go out with friends and have some freedom.
- S/he lets me spend money on myself.
- S/he lets me have personal space when I need it.

Workers should compare the partners' perceptions of each other. Where one person's high priority is the other person's low priority, this needs to be carefully examined by the worker.

Case study

Michelle's 'priority of relationship' statements about John

1. He looks after me.
2. Without him I would feel lonely.
3. I need a man in my life.
4. I do not want to start over again with someone else.
5. He is good with money.
6. I trust him.
7. He is better than my other partner.
8. He is a good friend.
9. He loves me.
10. He is a good parent.

John's 'priority of relationship' statements about Michelle

1. I trust her.
2. She lets me spend money on myself.
3. She lets me have personal space when I need it.
4. She is a good mother.

5. She looks after me.

6. She makes me feel wanted.

7. She loves me.

8. She is good with money.

Joint checklist on relationship issues

- Describe your relationship together year by year.

- What do you think are your strengths as a couple?

- What do you think are your weaknesses as a couple?

- What do you think you do best together?

- What are you worst at doing together?

- Describe a typical family day as a couple.

- How often do you disagree?

- What happens when you disagree?

- How often have you disagreed or argued when the child(ren) have been present?

- When you disagree about how to look after the child(ren), what happens?

- Who usually makes the important decisions about the child(ren)?

- How much time do you get to talk to each other?

- What do you talk about?

- How easy is it to talk to each other?

- How much time do you have together without the child(ren) around?

- Would you like to have more time alone together?

- What do you enjoy doing together most?

- Do you arrange for each other to have a break from the family and go out alone? If so, how often?

Case study

Responses to the 'checklist on relationship' discussion

John said that he and Michelle had been together for about eight months.

He said they had a good relationship and that they could look after David as well as any parents could.

He described their relationship strength as 'they worked well together' and their weakness as 'Michelle struggled to manage David and he had to give him some discipline'. When this was explored, John said that David gave Michelle the runaround and he ended up having to put David in his place. This was qualified as shouting at David so that he would do as he was told.

John said they did not have a typical day. Most days Michelle stayed at home while he hung around with his friends.

John said they disagreed when Michelle did not do as she was told, and Michelle agreed with this. When they disagree, John shouts at her.

They have disagreed in front of David, and when they do he usually becomes very quiet.

John said they usually disagreed about David because Michelle was too soft with him. He often has to tell her what to do.

John said he makes all of the decisions about David.

They do not talk to each other very often as John is out most of the time. When he is in they watch TV. They never go out together, as John likes going to the pub and Michelle does not.

John said that he goes out with his friends but Michelle does not get out, as she prefers to stay at home.

Training exercise/case study

There are case studies which look at the relationship with the current partner in the Appendix, Exercises 20.

2.19 PARENTING SKILLS AND ABILITIES

There are a number of different devices which can be used to assess parenting skills and abilities, depending on the specific circumstances of each case.

In some instances the 'safest' method is to consider a parenting or family assessment in a residential setting, and there are a number of such provisions. There is, of course, a disadvantage in placing parents and children away from where they live, perhaps for the first time in their lives:

- it places families in an environment where they may feel 'like being in a goldfish bowl', especially if there are video or audio monitoring arrangements in place

- it exposes children and parents to a new environment in which they may well react differently to the way they would at home

- it may have an unsettling effect on the emotional well-being of the child(ren)

- it may have an unsettling effect on the emotional well-being of the adults.

There are also advantages:

- it provides a safe environment during the assessment period

- it offers the opportunity to combine assessment with the development of parenting skills

- it allows for significantly greater periods of observation.

Practical parenting abilities can be tested by observation in the home or at a Family Centre. Even when observation in the home is the preferred option, the involvement of family centre staff may provide an additional expertise in the assessment process.

Be aware at all times that observation of the actions, interactions and responses of the children and parents provides valuable information for the assessment.

Whilst parents can often present a false perception of themselves, children are less likely to do so, less likely to be able to do so, or less prepared to do so.

It is more likely than not that the parents will attempt to show their 'best' parenting abilities during the assessment period.

The younger the child, the less likely it is that any behaviour is rehearsed, and the more likely that the behaviour represents an accurate picture.

However, the possibility of the worker or the assessment process having an impact on the child's behaviour should be considered.

The involvement of health visitors, midwives and medical personnel is helpful in putting together an understanding of whether children are, or have been, developing within normal limits whilst living at home.

The *Framework for the Assessment of Children in Need and their Families* (DoH 2000) provides the following materials which can be used with this practitioner's tool. They can be found in the 'Family Pack of Questionnaires and Scales':

- Parenting daily hassle

- Strengths and difficulties

- Family activity.

The *Framework for the Assessment of Children in Need and their Families*, Core Assessment Record (DoH 2000) also provides separate evaluation records within five age ranges: 0–2 years, 3–4 years, 5–9 years, 10–14 years and over 15 years. These are produced as individual booklets within the core assessment record. Within the area of parenting capacity the following areas of development needs are addressed:

- Health

- Education

- Emotional and behavioural development: self-care skills

- Identity and social presentation

- Family and social relationships.

Within each area of competence, parenting capacity is addressed under the following headings:

- Basic care

- Ensuring safety

- Emotional warmth

- Stimulation

- Guidance and boundaries

- Stability.

Within each of the core assessment records there is a checklist which addresses areas of competence and looks at the child's needs. This can also be used in conjunction with this practitioner's tool.

2.20 PERCEPTION OF CHILDREN

Gaining an understanding of the parents' perceptions of their child(ren) is crucial in identifying risk, making decisions and identifying appropriate action/resources needed.

Some adults have an idealised view of their child(ren) and this can lead to a failure to recognise, or refusal to acknowledge, potentially difficult behaviour, or to respond appropriately when the child(ren) are being, for example, naughty or destructive. Parents who believe, 'my child can do no wrong' are unlikely to establish appropriate boundaries for the child, who may develop uninhibited behaviour. The potential for future difficulties is real.

Adults who have a negative view of the child are likely to behave in an unsupportive, rejecting, dismissive or hostile fashion towards them. Children are likely to be under-stimulated and neglected. They will feel unloved and uncared-for.

If parents have a positive but realistic perception of children, they are likely to use good parenting strategies which will support and encourage the child. However, they will also use appropriate parental authority when they feel that behaviour or attitudes are not acceptable. The child(ren) will grow with a more balanced experience, fundamentally informed by the use of positive reinforcement, and this is more likely to lead to an emotionally healthy adult with a better capacity to develop good relationships and parent positively themselves.

There is discretion in the use of this checklist.

Checklist of parents'/carers' perception of the child

In respect of each child of the family:

Child's name.................

- Describe her/him.
- What do you think is the best thing about her/him?
- What do you think is the worst thing about her/him?
- What kind of things make her/him happy?
- When was the last time s/he was happy and why?
- Describe the happiest s/he has ever been in his/her life.
- How often do you think s/he is happy?
- What does s/he do when happy?
- How long does her/his happiness last?
- Is s/he happier now than when young? If not, why?

Explore other emotions in order to gain an understanding of the parents' perception of the child, for example:

- sadness
- anger
- despondency
- helplessness
- distress
- despair
- stress
- any other emotions.

Using the same questionnaire model, also explore behaviour, including the following:

- destructive

- uncontrollable

- defiant

- violent

- tantrums

- good

- constructive

- caring

- supportive

- any other behaviour.

When emotions and behaviours are being discussed, the impact on the person should be explored through the following additional questions:

- How does the behaviour make you feel?

- How do you respond to the behaviour?

- How does your partner respond?

- What kinds of behaviour does your child do differently with you than with your partner?

- How do the other children respond?

- How does the behaviour affect family life?

- What parts of your child's behaviour worry you?

- Are there parts of your child's behaviour which you feel unable to manage?

Case study

Michelle's perception of David

Michelle described David in the following terms:

'Brilliant.'

'I love him to bits.'

'He is a handful...really naughty...a little devil.'

'People say he can wind me round his little finger.'

'Sometimes when he looks at me, he looks just like his dad.'

'He is a pain when he won't go to bed.'

'He knows how to wind me up.'

'Most of the time he won't do as I tell him.'

'He can be really hurtful when he can't get his own way.'

'He lashes out at me sometimes.'

'He was always smiling when we lived at my grandmother's.'

She describes his best feature as 'He's a lovely little boy...he's mine,' and she least likes him when 'He has tantrums when he can't get his own way.'

Michelle feels David is happy when he gets his own way, which is most of the time with her. She was not able initially to say when David might have been at his happiest, but eventually concluded that it would have been when he was at home with her and her grandmother. When he is happy David tends to rush around, and John does not like that.

David is sad/unhappy when he cannot get his own way. She feels that is not very often with her, because 'I tend to spoil him and let him have his own way, but John is more strict with him.' She feels David is sad more often now than he used to be. He was extremely sad when his great-grandmother died, and she could not stop him crying. Most of the time when he is sad David comes to her for a cuddle, but sometimes he sits and cries. His sadness does not normally last long, except when John is in and makes David sit still.

David used to be angry quite a lot when he could not get his own way, but since John moved in his temper tantrums have almost disappeared. When they were living at Michelle's grandmother's, David would have angry outbursts quite often. Michelle found these difficult to manage and often gave in to him, but her grandmother would send him upstairs for a few minutes or ignore him, and this usually worked. Michelle does not know why David is angry less often since John came to live with them.

Michelle believes that David is a typical little lad, full of energy, mischief, into everything. He has tantrums like other children but he can be good when he wants and he can be very loving.

David's naughty behaviour, especially some of his tantrums, used to worry her, but these are now much less frequent and she feels happier. When he is contented she feels 'brilliant'.

She tries to spoil him when John is out because she thinks John can be a 'bit hard on him'. When he has a tantrum she tends to give in to him, as she does not like to see him upset.

Michelle says that John loves David really, but sometimes he has a lot on his mind and this makes him bad-tempered. He shouts at David sometimes. Michelle insists that she has not seen John hit David, and believes that he would never do that because he loves kids and would not do anything to hurt him.

Michelle feels that David is completely different when John is in the flat. 'He can be really lively and as soon as John comes in he goes really quiet.'

John's perception of David

John described David in the following terms:

> 'He's a pain.'

> 'He's forever moaning and getting under my feet.'

> 'Kids should be seen and not heard, that's how I had to be.'

> 'She spoils him rotten, Michelle, she'll ruin him if she gets her way.'

> 'He won't stand up for himself with other kids.'

> 'He is useless.'

John feels David is best 'when he is asleep', and worst 'when he is awake'.

John thinks David is happy when he is getting his own way and sad/angry when he is not. He blames Michelle for spoiling him and letting him get his own way too much. His view is that David needs a good dose of discipline and that will sort him out.

John believes that David has improved since he became a member of the household because of the discipline he has brought.

Training exercise/case study

There is a case study which looks at perception of children in the Appendix, Exercise 21.

2.21 PERCEPTION OF BEING A PARENT

Being a parent is the most complex, difficult and demanding task. It requires knowledge, patience, resilience and determination. Any weakness in a parent's physical and emotional energy is likely to be exposed by child care responsibilities and exploited by determined youngsters. The more children the person has to parent, the more demanding the task becomes.

Having looked at the person's perception of the child, explore their perception of themselves as a parent. This should include an understanding of parenting abilities, experiences, strengths and weaknesses. It should be related to the care of the child.

Workers should explore whether or not the person's perceptions result from their own experiences in childhood or whether they are formed from their experiences as a parent. In particular, if the person's perceptions mirror those of their parents, what is the likely result of that? For example, comments such as 'I got belted when I was naughty and it did not do me any harm', give indications of attitude and probable lack of insight into positive parenting strategies.

There is discretion in the use of this checklist.

Checklist for perceptions of parenting

- Is being a parent easy?
- What is the easiest thing about being a parent?
- What is the most difficult thing about being a parent?
- Do you like being a parent?
- What is the best thing about being a parent?

- What is the worst thing about being a parent?
- Is there anything about being a parent that you wish you could do better?
- What age of child do you feel most confident with?
- Is there a particular age of child you do not like or are not looking forward to? Why?
- What do you think is the most important thing you can offer your child(ren)?
- What do you do when your child cries?
- What kind of things do the child(ren) come to you for?
- What do you do when your child(ren) need(s) comforting?
- As a parent, do you think you have made any mistakes?
- What is the biggest mistake you think you have made as a parent?
- Has anything happened to your child(ren) which you regret?
- Do you feel school is important? If so, what do you do to help your child with schooling?

Case study

Michelle's perception of being a parent

Michelle believes being a parent is difficult.

She thinks the easiest thing is being able to love children and the most difficult is managing them when they are misbehaving, and the worry that they cause when they are ill.

She likes being a parent because David does not make her feel useless unlike the adults with whom she comes into contact. The worst thing is not having a minute to herself when David is around.

Michelle wishes she could manage David better than she does. She feels that sometimes she is running around after him all of the time and he is treating it like a game. She would like him to do things when she asks because then John would not end up shouting at both of them.

Michelle felt that she managed David best when he was a tiny baby, although she did have a lot of help from her grandmother.

She does not know what ages or stages she might find difficult, she accepts that she has very little experience as a parent. She thinks looking after a teenager might be hard.

Michelle thinks the most important thing she can offer David is not to smack him as he is growing up. She feels if she did that, David would stop loving her.

When David cries, Michelle tries to give him a cuddle. This works sometimes but not always. She finds that if he keeps on crying that makes her upset and she tends to give in to him.

She finds that David usually comes to her when he wants something. Occasionally he comes for a cuddle and that makes Michelle feel good.

Michelle recognises that she has made lots of mistakes. The biggest mistake is that she has let David get away with too much and he expects to get his own way all of the time.

She regrets that he is not living at home now and that he has been hurt.

Michelle thinks that school is very important and she would do everything she could to ensure David attended. She recognises that she would not be able to help with his schooling because she is not good at reading and writing.

John's perception of being a parent

John considers that being a parent is easy.

He does not think there is anything about being a parent that is difficult. He expects children to do as they are told and if they do not, then he would make them. When this was explored he offered the following strategies:

- smack their backsides
- shout at them
- send them to bed
- let them know who the boss is.

When the issue of physical chastisement was explored, John explained that 'I got many a good hiding when I was young and it didn't do me any harm.'

John did not consider anything particularly good about being a parent – nor, for that matter, anything which was particularly bad. It is his view that 'Children should be seen and not heard, and preferably not seen', and so long as that happens there are no problems.

John does not believe that he would do anything different. He considers himself to be a competent parent who needs no additional skills.

He feels confident with all ages of children, although he is looking forward to them as they get older so that he can show them 'the tricks of the trade'. He was not prepared to expand on this comment.

John feels the most important thing he can give to children is to show them how to look after themselves so that people do not take advantage, and how to stand up for themselves. Otherwise they end up like Michelle, everyone wipes their feet on her when he is not around.

Children cry because they are weak and pathetic. They need to learn how to be tough. John feels that cuddles are a sign of parental weakness and that children take advantage of that.

John does not feel he has made any mistakes as a parent except that he allowed the social workers to take David into care, and he regrets that.

School is important, but being able to look after yourself, not be cheated or taken advantage of by other people, is more important.

Training exercise/case study

There is a case study which looks at perceptions of parenting in the Appendix, Exercise 22.

2.22 PARENTING AND STRESS

Parenting is stressful, and the extent to which that is so should be explored. The first checklist looks at what other stresses the person has in their life and how they cope with stress generally.

The second checklist looks specifically at the stress of parenting, and in detail at the stress of parenting the parent's own particular children. Where there is more than one child in the family the checklist can be tested against the children as a sibling group, each child of the family, or the child considered to be the one most likely to cause stress.

These checklists should be applied in their entirety in order to gain the fullest understanding.

Checklist for stress

- Do you think you are someone who suffers from stress?
- What kind of things make you feel stressed?
- Does any group of people make you feel stressed?
- Do any individuals make you feel stressed?
- Does the child(ren) make you feel stressed sometimes?
- What things do they do which make you feel stressed?
- Describe how you feel when you are stressed.
- How often do you feel stressed?
- What is the most stress you have ever been under?
- What do you do when you feel stressed?
- Have you ever been to the doctor because of stress?
- Have you ever been on medication because of stress?
- What does your partner do when you are stressed?
- Does this help or make things worse?
- Is there anything which helps to reduce your stress?

Checklist on parental stress

- Do you find being a parent stressful?
- Is your child so active that sometimes you feel really tired?
- Does your child do things to wind you up?
- Does your child break things?
- Do you find your child is more difficult than most children?

- If your child really wants something do they go on and on until they get it?
- Do you think your child does things sometimes to please you?
- Does your child enjoy playing with you?
- Is your child often miserable and unhappy?
- Is being a parent harder than you thought it would be?
- Does your child lose his/her temper over silly little things?
- Does your child learn things quickly?
- Do you think that your child demands more of you than most other children?
- Does your child do as s/he is told?
- Do you think your child behaves better at school than at home?
- Is your child usually in a good mood in the morning?
- Does your child always seem to want money for something?
- Are there things about your child's behaviour which make you angry?
- Are there times when you do not feel particularly close to your child?
- Have you found looking after your child(ren) more difficult than you thought it would be?

Case study

Michelle's responses on stress

Michelle believes that she does suffer from stress, and takes tablets prescribed by her doctor to help her to keep calm. She has been on the tablets for a few years.

Lots of things make her feel anxious and stressed, for example, when she is left in the house alone or when John is shouting at her.

She does not like it when too many people are around or there is a lot of noise. When John's friends are at the flat she feels tense. She feels very stressed when the social workers come to see her. The most stress she has ever felt was when they told her at the hospital that David had been injured and when her grandmother died.

David sometimes made Michelle feel stressed when he was being really naughty and this was the main reason she went to see the doctor.

Some days Michelle feels stressed all of the time and cannot wait to go to bed so that the feelings will go away.

When she feels stressed Michelle sits by herself and tries to calm down. When this does not work she sometimes cries.

Usually when she feels stressed, John ignores her or tells her to 'stop being stupid'. Her grandmother used to talk to her and she found that this helped.

Michelle's parenting stress checklist responses

- Michelle feels that being a parent is very stressful.

- David tires her out sometimes with his energy and demands.

- He winds her up all of the time.

- He breaks things all the time, but he is only four years old.

- She finds David more difficult than other people find their children.

- David goes on until he gets what he wants. He throws tantrums if Michelle says no.

- Sometimes David does things to please Michelle. He cuddles her sometimes if she cries and that makes her feel better.

- David gets annoyed if Michelle refuses to play with him.

- David is always unhappy when he cannot get his own way.

- Being a parent is much harder than Michelle thought it would be.

- David loses his temper over silly things.

- He does learn quickly when he concentrates on something.

- The most stressful thing about being a parent is all the responsibility.

- David is more demanding than other children. Michelle blames herself for that. She should have been more strict with him.

- David rarely does as he is told.

- When he was at nursery David always behaved much better than at home.

- He could be in a good mood in the morning.

- David is too young to have money but he always wants sweets and toys which Michelle cannot afford.

- Sometimes Michelle does get angry with the way David goes on at her.

- Sometimes she does not feel close to David.

- She has found looking after David a lot more difficult than she expected.

John's responses on stress

John does not consider that he suffers from very much stress. He believes that stress is all in the mind and he has a strong mind.

The only thing he has felt stressed about in the past few years has been the social workers taking David away for no reason.

Stress makes him feel angry.

He has never been under the doctor for stress although he was prescribed sleeping tablets some years ago in prison. They said he was suffering from stress but he was not.

John's parenting stress checklist responses

- Being a parent is not stressful.

- David does not tire John out, because he makes David sit still.

- David dare not do anything to wind John up, because he knows what will happen.

- David breaks things all the time and this annoys John.

- David is no more difficult than other children once he knows who is the boss.

- David never pesters John for things.

- He never does things to please John. He keeps out of his way.

- John does not let David play with him.

- David is not particularly miserable.

- Being a parent is easier than John thought. He does not know what all the fuss is about, it comes naturally to him.

- David does lose his temper over little things but not when John is around.

- He is probably a bright kid but he acts stupid.

- Nothing is stressful.

- David does not make any demands.

- He always does as John tells him.

- He is not as good at nursery school as he is when he is at home with John.

- John does not know what David is like in the morning. He is always asleep.

- David never wants anything from John.

- David used to make John angry, but not now, since he started doing as he is told.

- John feels that David looks up to him and they get on great now.

- Looking after children is not difficult.

Training exercise/case study

There are case studies which look at parenting and stress in the Appendix, Exercises 23 and 24.

2.23 PARENTING AND THE NEEDS OF CHILDREN

The next stage is to look at the person's knowledge about parenting. The following questions look at the person's understanding of a child's physical needs, emotional needs, knowledge about basic child development and age-appropriate activities/responsibilities. It also explores their perceptions about what children should and should not be allowed to do at certain ages.

This checklist is of most benefit if it is applied in its entirety.

Checklist for parenting knowledge and style

- Why do babies cry?
- How would you respond to the different types of crying?
- What physical needs does a child have as s/he is growing up?
- What emotional needs does a child have as s/he is growing up?
- What educational needs does a child have as s/he is growing up?
- How do you think children learn?
- What kind of things do you think are naughty?
- What things can a parent do when a child is naughty?
- Would you ever smack your child? If so, what for?
- Do you think children like to be cuddled? If so, when would you cuddle them?
- Do you think that children should know that parents are 'in charge'?
- If so, how would you let your children know you were in charge?
- Should parents encourage imaginary play with small children, for example, having a tea party?
- Should parents join in?
- At what age do you think children would want to stop playing at having tea parties or imaginary play?
- How often do you think parents should play with children?
- How long do you think a child of 12 months will concentrate on one game/thing/activity –
  - one minute
  - five minutes

- ten minutes

- fifteen minutes

- thirty minutes

- forty-five minutes?

- Why do you think they can concentrate for that long?

- At what age do you think children should be allowed to go to the shop alone?

- When should children be allowed to have boyfriends/girlfriends?

- When should children be allowed to stay up until 10.00pm?

- At what age should children be allowed to stay in the house alone?

- At what age should children be allowed in the kitchen unsupervised?

- At what age should children be allowed a say in important family decisions – for example, whether a new partner should be allowed to move into the house?

- How old should children be before they are allowed pocket money?

- How old should a child be before they are told about contraception, masturbation, safe sex?

- Is there an age when you think children should be allowed to watch pornographic films?

Case study

Michelle's parenting knowledge and style

Michelle thinks that babies cry because they are tired, hungry, want their nappy changed or want to be cuddled. She would see what the problem was and deal with it.

A growing child needs to be looked after, fed and have proper clothes. They should never be neglected. They should be given lots of love and attention so that they are never lonely or frightened.

Children learn by going to school. There are no other ways which Michelle could think of through which children learn.

Michelle thinks that most children are naughty some of the time and that is all right. However, if they are naughty all of the time there must be a reason. The reason might be because there is something wrong or their parents are not being strict enough with them.

If a child is naughty the parent can send them to bed, stop their pocket money, tell them it is naughty or make them stay in if they are older. She does not think there would be any time when children should be hit. She has never smacked David and she never would.

She feels that children do like to be cuddled, not only when they are hurt but just to know they are loved.

Children should know that the parents are in charge. Michelle thinks this is a problem for her and sometimes she loses control of David's behaviour. She is not sure how she could be in control of David. She has tried shouting like John does but this does not work for her. She feels things are better now because John makes David do as he is told.

Michelle is not sure whether children should be encouraged with pretend play, but she does this all the time with David and he enjoys it. She thinks they should stop imaginary play before they go to school.

A one-year-old would only be able to concentrate on one thing for a short time, probably one minute, because something else will attract their attention.

Michelle feels children should be allowed to go to the shops alone when they have started school.

David should have a girlfriend when he is at the comprehensive school.

He should stay up until 10 o'clock, be allowed in the kitchen, and in the house alone, and allowed pocket money, when he starts at the comprehensive school.

She does not think David should be involved in decisions such as whether or not someone else should come to live in the flat.

She does not know when he should learn about sex, etc., and should never watch pornographic films. She would ask John when these things should happen.

John's parenting knowledge and style

John thinks babies cry when they want something.

When they are very small someone has to tend to them, but they should be taught to do things for themselves as soon as possible.

John feels that children should be taught to stand on their own two feet as soon as possible. Loving and cuddles makes children soft and that is what has happened to David. School is okay and John recognises its value. However, John feels that David could learn a lot from him about life.

Children learn from being told what to do.

When they are naughty, children should be sorted out by the parents. This could include being told off, sent to bed, having pocket money stopped or not being allowed to watch TV. John did not feel that children should be rewarded for good behaviour, they should behave themselves anyway.

Children who are naughty should also be smacked. He thinks naughty includes not doing as they are told, swearing and answering back. John was smacked when he was a child and he feels it has not done him any harm.

John thinks it is important for children to know that parents are in charge. David knows that, John has told him many times.

John did not think children should be allowed to pretend-play, and he would not join in anything like that.

A twelve-month-old would be able to concentrate for a minute at most because they are easily distracted.

Children should be allowed to do things when the parents thought they were old enough, sensible enough or deserved to be allowed to do things. He felt it depended, as some children are mature much sooner than others.

John felt that children should know about sex, etc. as soon as they would understand, and that there was nothing wrong with them watching pornography when they were old enough to understand about sex.

Training exercise/case study

There is a case study on parenting knowledge and style in the Appendix, Exercise 25.

2.24 THE CHILD

This tool is not intended for assessing the child. However, there are a number of fundamental issues worthy of comment.

How information is collected in respect of the child depends upon the child's age and understanding, the availability of information, and access to that information.

The worker should first of all establish whether or not the child is of sufficient age and understanding to have an informed view on matters pertinent to his/her physical and emotional well-being.

Where children are of sufficient age and understanding, the 'Core Assessment Record' booklet can be used as the basis for discussion, and may be used in checklist form, as applicable to various development needs.

If children are not of sufficient age and understanding, the 'Core Assessment Record' booklet can be used as an assessment checklist by the worker.

Earlier parts of the assessment will have gained substantial information about the child, and this should be considered within the context of further information that is required within this section.

Consult with other agencies about the child, and incorporate any information which they are able to provide. Health visitors, paediatricians, doctors, midwives, teachers, youth workers, police, child protection workers in other departments and organisations, are representative of other services which may have been involved in the child's life.

Observation of family life, the actions and interactions of the child and their family, also provide a valuable source of understanding about the child and their needs.

In observing the behaviour of the child and the family's management of that behaviour, it may be helpful to check actions, reactions and interactions within a specific period. The following checklist for monitoring parental response, identifies these issues within a specific time-scale. It provides information on the parenting style, the extent of the person's ability to maintain a predominant child care focus, and the nature of the relationship between the child and the adult. The checklist can be used a number of times throughout the assessment to give a more accurate picture.

Checklist for monitoring parental response

Proactive/reactive parent/child interactions [tick for each interaction]

Interaction between...

Date ....

Time ....

Parent appropriately proactive.

Positive response from child.

Negative response from child.

Parent inappropriately proactive with the child.

Parent reacted appropriately to the child.

Parent made inappropriate/negative response to the child.

Parent failed to respond to the child.

Signed ....Date ....Time ....

2.25 ATTACHMENT

The assessment of the child's attachment to their primary carer should be included in the assessment. The assessment of attachment involves observation of the child and parent throughout the entire period of the assessment.

The *Framework for the Assessment of Children in Need and their Families*, Reader, Chapter 12, 'Attachment' (DoH 2000) can be used in conjunction with this practice tool. There are four patterns of attachment within the parent/child relationship which are identified in the reader:

- **Secure attachment** is seen where the parent is available to the child, positively responsive, nurturing, caring and loving. Children are able to explore their world with confidence, achieve their full potential, have a good self-worth and self-esteem, trust others, and cope better with social and interpersonal situations. They grow up in an emotionally healthy manner. Children who have been securely attached to their primary carers are more likely to develop secure attachments to their own children.

- **Ambivalent attachment** is seen where the parent is unpredictable, inconsistent and neglectful in behaviour and response, sometimes welcoming and supportive and at other times negative and rejecting. Parents will be low on acceptance, sensitivity and availability and high on neglect.

  They frequently fail to empathise with the child's needs, feelings and moods. Parents tend to respond to children when it satisfies their emotional need rather than the child's emotional need. Love comes to the child in a totally unpredictable manner. The child is uncertain what to expect and is therefore likely to demand parental attention and reject it at the same time, never able to trust the parent's reaction. Children have poor self-esteem and self-confidence, place little value on themselves, feel helpless and appear dependent. Hyperactive behaviour is a typical pattern.

- **Avoidant attachment** is seen where the parent is rejecting, hostile and intrusive. Although the parent may respond reasonably well when the child is behaving well and not causing them any difficulties, they will become distant, unavailable and rejecting if the child becomes distressed, needs attention or comforting. There is a deactivation of caregiving behaviour, including 'backing off' by the parent and resentment towards the child. The child is likely to show little emotional connection to the parent, become self-reliant, self-contained and independent. The child will either become compliant (to avoid behaviour which may lead to rejection) or become a 'loner'. When separated from parents the child will demonstrate little, if any, distress.

- **Disorganised attachment** is seen where the parent is not exclusively hostile and rejecting, but at times their behaviour is frightening to the child and may be dangerous. Some parents may be unable to provide an emotional connection/commitment to the child because of the impact of drugs/alcohol/substance abuse, unresolved trauma, or mental ill-health. This emotional unavailability causes the child to become anxious – therefore, wanting to go to the parent for comfort. However, the potential source of comfort is also the person who causes the anxiety. This is a problem the child is unable to resolve. Children typically become confused and distressed. Restless, agitated behaviour is evident within relationships. They present as disturbed, socially isolated and frequently aggressive.

Ambivalent, avoidant and disorganised attachments are all insecure forms of attachment.

2.26 HOME ENVIRONMENT

Assess whether or not the home environment is suitable for the safe care of children and whether or not systems exist to manage the home on a daily basis. Questions can be asked directly or conclusions drawn by the worker throughout the assessment.

This tool recommends a checklist in respect of the physical conditions within the home. Issues of safety can also be addressed by way of a checklist, as appropriate.

The *Framework for the Assessment of Children in Need and their Families*, 'The Family Pack of Questionnaires: Home Conditions' (DoH 2000) can be used in conjunction with this tool.

Workers can use discretion with this checklist.

Checklist for living arrangements

- How many rooms are there downstairs?
- How many bedrooms are there?
- What are the sleeping arrangements?
- Is there a place in the house where some privacy can be achieved?
- What is the level of general cleanliness in the house?
- Are there any specific areas of the house which are unacceptable?
- How are the household cleaning arrangements organised?
- Are there any particular difficulties in keeping the house clean and tidy?
- Do the children have sufficient appropriate clothing?
- Do the adults have sufficient appropriate clothing?
- How often are clothes washed?
- Is there equipment to do laundry? If not, how is it done?
- Is there sufficient bedding, in good condition?
- How often is the bedding washed?
- Are there facilities to dry the clothes?
- Is the furniture sufficient and in reasonable condition?
- Who does the shopping?
- Who usually cooks?
- Is the diet varied and balanced?
- What food has been consumed in the last three days?
- Does the family usually live on convenience foods?
- Is the kitchen clean and tidy?
- Is the cooker adequate?
- Is there a fridge? If not, how are foods kept safely?
- Is there a freezer?

- Are the parents aware of safety issues?
- Are the following safety issues addressed?
  - medicines
  - kitchen dangers
  - fireguards
  - socket protectors
  - inflammable substances
  - electrical equipment
  - matches and lighters
  - drugs and equipment
  - alcohol
  - sharp instruments
  - stair-gates
  - cleaning materials

Case study

Living Arrangements

The flat is on the first floor above some shops. The staircase is narrow and there is no lighting.

There is a lounge, kitchen, bathroom and two bedrooms. When David was at home he had his own bedroom.

The flat is small and privacy is difficult to achieve.

The flat is untidy and usually dirty. From time to time Michelle makes an effort to improve conditions, but John's friends tend to leave it in a mess when they have visited. There is no vacuum-cleaner.

The bathroom is very dirty. The bath is broken and personal cleanliness is therefore difficult. The furniture is in poor condition. The bedrooms have no furniture apart from a bed.

David was appropriately clothed when he was living at home, although he was often undressed during visits.

There have been times when Michelle has not worn clothing appropriate to the conditions. She has no coat and her shoes are in a poor state of repair.

There is no washing-machine and, because the bath is broken, no means of washing clothes at the flat. Michelle said that she sometimes goes to the launderette. The bedding is often dirty and soiled.

John said that he decides what shopping is needed and Michelle goes and gets it. They tend to shop day by day and there is little food kept in the house because they have no fridge.

Only the top of the cooker works but they do not have elaborate meals. Their diet consists mainly of sandwiches and convenience foods. They have eaten pizzas in recent days.

There are problems of hygiene in the kitchen mainly because of the poor levels of cleanliness. John says that this is because Michelle does not know how to keep the flat clean.

The flat does have a fireguard and there is a stairgate at the flat door. The electrical equipment is in poor condition and there are regular interruptions when fuses blow. None of the sockets in the kitchen works.

Michelle does have a cupboard in the kitchen where she keeps things out of David's reach. She does worry sometimes because John and his friends leave used needles around in the lounge.

Training exercise/case study
There is an exercise on living arrangements in the Appendix, Exercise 26.

2.27 FINANCES
Lack of money is frequently a cause of tension and argument within families. Debt is one of the leading causes of stress.

The way in which the income of the family is spent is frequently an indicator of the priorities within the family. For example, parents may spend money on drugs instead of food for the children. It can also indicate the construction of relationships. For example, one partner may see funding their night out with friends as a better use of resources than their partner's bus fare to visit family.

The following information on finances is needed. The worker has discretion in the use of this checklist.

Checklist for finances

- What is the family income?
- How is the income made up?
- How is the income spent?
- What are the family's financial priorities?
- What happens to any money left over?
- What are the family debts?
- How are these debts being managed?
- Are any of the debts critical?

Case study

Finances

Michelle and John claim their state benefits separately.

John takes responsibility for all finances and gives Michelle money for specific things like food.

The majority of the money is spent on drugs and alcohol.

They are in arrears with the rent and owe a debt on the electricity supply. John refused to give details of the extent of their debts and indicated that their debt problems would soon be resolved.

Training exercise/case study

There is an exercise on finances in the Appendix, Exercise 27.

2.28 CHILD PROTECTION CONCERNS

The parents' understanding of professional concerns about the care and well-being of the child(ren) should be explored.

Each incident of concern, including injuries, should be explored with the family. An understanding of how any injuries occurred is important to the assessment.

Denial of blame or responsibility for injuries, or a refusal to accept concerns about the care of the children, is a negative indicator to safe care in the future.

Where the issue is one of long-term, cumulative concerns, issues such as emotional harm or neglect, or a child protection incident, the following checklist should be used. The checklist should be applied so that all concerns are explored in detail and an understanding of the person's views, feelings and attitudes is obtained.

Checklist for child protection concerns

- What do you think are the concerns for your child?
- Why do you think people are concerned?
- Do you think all of the concerns are real?
- Do you think any of the concerns are real?
- Do you think your child has suffered in any way?
- Do you think things should be different?
- If so, what things should be different?

Where there is expert evidence, for example, medical evidence to support the concerns, parents should be made aware of this and have the opportunity to respond. The following should be discussed:

- What happened?
- Do you think you or your partner did anything wrong?
- Did you injure the child in any way?
- If you did not injure the child, do you think your partner did?
- If the same situation arose again would you do anything differently?
- Do you do anything different now to prevent something like that happening again?
- Did you learn anything from what happened?

Case study

Local authority concerns

Michelle thinks that the social workers are concerned because she finds it difficult sometimes to look after David, and that is why they have visited her since he was born.

John stated that the social services department has visited since he and Michelle started to live together because they interfere in people's lives and take their children away from them and because Michelle cannot keep David under control.

He does not believe that the concerns in any way involve him.

Previous concerns by social workers in respect of his daughter Aimee were because Dianne A was a drug addict and was not looking after Aimee properly.

Michelle feels they have co-operated with the social workers in the months leading up to the injuries which David sustained. John reported his non-co-operation was due to the fact that the social workers had 'caused nothing but trouble', and were always trying to tell him what to do.

John says they look after David all right. He knows lots of families where the parents are out of their head on drugs and do not look after their children as well as David is looked after and no-one does anything about that. The social workers have got their claws into him and Michelle and will not be happy until David is adopted.

John insists there is nothing to worry about with David, he is fine now that he does as he is told.

John believes they should have somewhere better to live.

Michelle does not know how David's injuries occurred. He was all right when she went to bed but in the morning his arm was really swollen. John told her he must have fallen or something.

John's opinion is that David must have fallen badly. He remembers that he and some of his friends were 'messing about' with David after Michelle had gone to bed, but David was enjoying it and joining in. John qualified 'messing about' as having 'fun fights with him and throwing him from one to the other'. John believes that is a good way to toughen David up.

Michelle insists that she has never hit or hurt David.

John insists that he has never hurt David. He accepts that he has given him the 'odd tap' when he has been naughty in the past, but he does not have to do that now as he only has to give him a look and David does as he is told.

John thinks that David is a clumsy lad who falls over a lot and is always picking up bumps and bruises.

Michelle thinks that David must have fallen awkwardly. She does not believe that John would do anything to hurt David, he is not that sort of person.

John feels the only lesson they have learned is not to let doctors and social workers get their hands on children as they make up lies to have them adopted.

Training exercise/case study

There is a case study which looks at child protection in the Appendix, Exercise 28.

2.29 EVALUATING THE INFORMATION

Collecting the information is one aspect of the assessment. Evaluating and interpreting that information enables decisions to be made about how best to safeguard and promote the welfare of the children.

> Research, the findings of Inquiry Reports and Social Service Inspectorate inspections, have frequently highlighted weaknesses in this area of assessment. A great deal of time and effort goes into the information gathering stage. This results in an assessment that focuses on describing what is happening. However, often less attention is given to the analysis of the information gathered. (DoH 2000, 'Guidance Notes and Glossary for Core Assessment Record', p.10.)

This tool places a clear emphasis on systematic evaluation of the information which has been collected. The following checklists are designed to ensure that the information is comprehensively analysed and recorded in the assessment document. The checklists are not exhaustive, and workers are encouraged to use them in a flexible way, depending on the needs of each case.

Checklist for profile

- How did the person present during the assessment?
- Which sessions, if any, were difficult?
- What was the level of co-operation?
- Was the co-operation different from that seen in other assessments? If so, why?
- Were any special arrangements needed, for example interpreter, supporter, etc?
- What level of competence does s/he have? (Comments should be confined to known assessments by professionals, for example psychiatrists or psychologists.)
- How was account taken of levels of competence – for example, the use of limited language in the case of a person with learning difficulty, or the use of specific assessment material?
- What was the person's overall presentation? Within what range of behaviour was the person usually seen? Was the person **passive**, **submissive**, **assertive**, **dominant**, **hostile**, **aggressive**, and what does this mean in terms of:
  - their ability to manage
  - their relationship ability and capacity
  - their child care abilities, including child protection?
- Did the person respond with different behaviour in different situations, and what does this mean in terms of:
  - their ability to manage
  - their relationship ability and capacity
  - their child care ability and capacity?
- Did the person respond with different behaviour when relating or responding to different people and what does this mean in terms of:
  - their ability to manage
  - their relationship ability and capacity
  - their child care ability and capacity?

- Within the range of overall presentation, what other aspects of behaviour were evident, and what is the effect of this?

- Is anything known about the person's mental health?

- Is anything known about the person through psychological assessment?

- Is there any other expert opinion about the person?

- Is there any significant medical information about the person which has an impact on the person's life?

- Does drug or alcohol abuse have a significant impact on the person's life?

- Are there any significant issues of anger or violence?

- At what level is the person's self-esteem?

- How well does the person manage within the community? Are particular strategies used, and how successful are these?

- Does the person require external support systems to sustain them in the community?

- Are the person's current social, personal and interpersonal arrangements likely to continue? If so, why?

- What are the significant aspects/behaviours of the person, and how do these impact on their ability to function?

- Describe any negative or positive indicators which would impact on the ability to safeguard and promote the welfare of children.

Checklist for experiences from childhood

A person' s experiences from childhood provide information about:

- what kind of childhood they had

- their parents' skills and abilities

- the type of adult relationships they witnessed

- the child care management systems they experienced

- the extent to which their physical, emotional and developmental needs were satisfied

- what kinds of attachments they had to their primary carers

- the lessons they learned from childhood.

Checklist

- Describe the overall arrangements of childhood care. For example, was the person brought up exclusively by parents, were the arrangements varied, were there any episodes in care?

- What was the person's perception of each parent?

- What was the relationship with each parent?

- What was the relationship with any significant others?

- What are relationships like now?

- What relationship did the person have with siblings?

- What is that relationship like now?

- What is the evidence of good care, love, appropriate affection, nurturing or other positive emotional experiences?

- What is the evidence of rejection, isolation, loneliness, abandonment, or any other negative experiences?

- What was the likely level of attachment?

- Are there any childhood experiences which are likely to have caused significant harm, or which indicate, unsafe care?

- Describe the relationship between the person's parents.

- What was the individual parenting style of the parents?

- Was the parenting style complementary or did styles and actions contradict each other?

- What was the effect of the joint parenting?

- Were there any deficiencies in one parent's abilities which were compensated for by the other parent?

- Were any parenting strategies abusive?

- Were the behaviour management strategies positive or negative?

- Are the person's childhood experiences positive or negative?

- How has the person internalised those experiences? For example, being hit as a child may lead to the use of similar systems ('I was hit and it never did me any harm') or a determination not to hit children.

- Do the person's childhood experiences have a significant impact on current behaviour?

- Are there any unresolved issues from childhood which have an impact on the person's emotional well-being, ability to function or ability as a parent?

- Are the person's perceptions of childhood realistic? If not, how does this impact on their view of parenting?

Checklist for parenting skills and abilities

a) **In terms of a general overview of parenting skills:**

- Does the person have a good enough understanding of a child's physical needs at various stages throughout childhood? If not, give examples.

- Is the person able to provide for the child's physical needs? If not, give examples.

- Does the person provide a good enough level of basic care? If not, in what ways?

- How is the person able to keep a child safe from harm, hazards or danger, including:
  - unsafe care
  - contact with unsafe people
  - home and environment safety
  - safety from self-harm?

- Does the person have a good enough understanding of a child's emotional needs at various stages throughout childhood? If not, in what areas? Give examples.

- Is the person able to provide for the emotional needs of the child(ren)? If not, in what areas? Give examples.

- Have there been any previous concerns regarding the person's parenting?

- What is the person's parenting experience?
- Is there anything about the person's parenting skills and style which places the child at risk of significant harm?

b) **In terms of the specific child**:

- Describe the person's relationship with the child.
- Does the person provide a stable, settled, consistent environment for the child?
- Is there evidence of good enough physical care?
- Is there evidence of the appropriate use of parental authority?
- Is there evidence of emotional warmth?
- What is the level of attachment between the child and parent?
- Does the person respond appropriately to the child's emotional needs?
- Does the child present particular difficulties which the person does not recognise?
- How would the person deal with difficult behaviour?
- What methods of behaviour management/discipline would the person use?
- Does the person use positive reinforcement or negative sanction in respect of the child's behaviour?
- Does the person find parenting the child stressful?
- How is the person likely to respond in a crisis?
- Does the person have the overall skills and ability to parent the child?
- Is the person able to prioritise the needs of the child over their own needs at all times?
- Does the person have the physical and emotional resources to parent the child safely at all times?

c) **In terms of the combined parenting skills and abilities**:

- Are there parenting skills/styles in one parent which compensate for lack of skills in the other parent?

- What aspects, if any, of the combined parenting skills/styles complement each other?

- What aspects, if any, of the combined parenting skills/styles contradict each other, and what impact does this have on the care of the child? Give examples.

- Do the combined skills/styles and abilities enable a good enough, safe enough level of care to be maintained?

- Are there any relationship issues which impact on the parenting skills and abilities?

- Are there any relationship difficulties which place the child(ren) at risk of significant harm?

- Is the person or are the couple able to parent the child(ren) in ways which would always safeguard and promote their welfare?

Checklist for drugs, alcohol, substance abuse

Where drugs, alcohol or substance misuse are an issue, the following additional analysis should be included:

- Is there enough money to ensure the child(ren)'s needs are met?

- Are the person's needs more important to them than the needs of the child(ren)?

- Is there a difference in the level of care provided at times when the person is intoxicated?

- Does the other parent/partner also have a habit?

- Are adequate arrangements made for the child(ren) during periods of intoxication?

- Do these arrangements keep the child(ren) safe?

- Is the physical environment safe – for instance, are drugs or used needles accessible to the child(ren)? Is equipment kept safe?

- Do other users frequent the house and become intoxicated?

- Does the drug/alcohol/substance misuse disrupt the daily routines?

Checklist for Schedule 1 offences

- How do the offences impact on the person's ability to provide safe care for the child(ren)?

- Has the person attended any courses for Schedule 1 offenders, and has that reduced the level of risk?

- Does the person continue to deny the offences, and what conclusions are drawn from that?

- Is the person's partner able to protect the child(ren)?

- Are there any systems which can be introduced which will ensure the safe care of the child(ren)?

Checklist for relationship between parents

- Describe the relationship between the parents/adults.

- What advantages and disadvantages does the relationship offer to each person?

- Are there particular aspects of the relationship which have an impact on child care issues?

- Are there any significant relationship difficulties?

- What is likely to happen to the relationship in the future?

Checklist on health, criminal history, finances and other issues

- What is the significance of the information in terms of the ability to provide for the safe care of child(ren)?

Checklist for the child(ren)

The assessment of the child's needs can be completed using the checklist provided in the appropriate Core Assessment Records (DoH 2000).

Where the assessment is to be used as part of court proceedings, the assessment can follow the Children Act 1989, Section 1 (3), which is referred to as the welfare checklist:

a)   the ascertainable wishes and feelings of the child concerned (considered in the light of his/her age and understanding)

b)   his/her physical, emotional and educational needs

c)   the likely effect on him/her of any change in circumstances

d)   his/her age, sex and background and any characteristics of him/her which the court considers relevant

e)   any harm which s/he has suffered or is likely to suffer.

The assessment should address the following issues:

- Are the child(ren)'s physical and developmental needs being met?

- Is/are the child(ren) reaching developmental milestones?

- If the child(ren) is/are a baby, are basic care needs of feeding, bathing, physical care being provided?

- Are the child(ren)'s immunisations up to date?

- Is the child(ren)'s clothing adequate and appropriate to weather conditions?

- Is the child(ren)'s bedding adequate and clean?

- Are the child(ren)'s health care needs met?

- Is/are the child(ren) referred to the GP appropriately?

- Are health care appointments missed?

- Is/are the child(ren) provided with appropriate stimulation?

- Are there sufficient age-appropriate toys available?

- Are speech and language developing within normal limits?

- Are the child(ren)'s educational needs being met?

- Does/do the child(ren) have an appropriate daily routine?

- Is/are the child(ren) provided with a positive emotional climate?

- Are the child(ren)'s emotional needs being met?

- Is the child(ren)'s interaction with others positive?

- Is the child(ren)'s relationship with others helpful to his/her emotional well-being?

- Are there any significant behaviours which give rise for concern?

- Does/do the child(ren) have a good relationship with primary carers?

- What is the attachment between the child(ren) and carers?

- Does/do the child(ren) present as self-confident?

- Does/do the child(ren) have good self-esteem?

- Does/do the child(ren) have age-appropriate levels of competence?

- Has/have the child(ren) suffered significant harm?

- Is/are the child(ren) at risk of suffering significant harm?

Checklist for child protection concerns and the capacity to change

Whether or not parents are able to look after their children in ways which will safeguard and promote their welfare is determined by analysis of all the information which is known about the family.

Issues of significant harm, an understanding of the individual profile and behaviour of the adults, their existing relationships, their parenting ability, the needs of the children, and whether or not those needs can be met by the parents, all contribute to that analysis.

Also important is an understanding of the parents' ability to change. What exists at present may place the children at risk of significant harm. If, however, changes can be made within an appropriate time-scale, it may be possible to put in place safeguards which would allow the family to remain together whilst essential work is undertaken. Alternatively, it may be possible for work to be undertaken towards rehabilitation within a time-scale which would be appropriate to the needs of the children.

In addressing the issue of change, the assessment should apply the principle that any delay may be prejudicial to the best interests of the children. This is particularly important where the permanent placement of children away from their parents (adoption) is one of the options. The sooner children move into such placements, the sooner they may be able to get on with the process of growing up, making attachments and recovering from any unhelpful childhood experiences.

Treacher and Carpenter (1989) suggest that parents should make three basic statements indicative of their motivation to change:

- I have a problem regarding the behaviour of myself or another which distresses me.

- I have tried to solve this problem alone, or with the help of others, and these problem-solving attempts have been unsuccessful.

- I am asking for help.

The 'comprehensive model of change' produced by Prochaska and DiClemente (1991) can be applied to identify the following stages:

- **pre-contemplation** usually occurs at the initial stages of intervention by the child protection agencies. Families typically respond with defensive behaviour and are resistant to the notion of change. Frequently they are reluctant to look at the issues of concern.

- **contemplation** is achieved when the parents recognise that there is perhaps a need for change. Acknowledging issues and understanding what needs to change often helps this process. The family begins to think seriously about change and feel strongly that there is a need to change.

- **action** comes when parents make the decision to change. They will respond when clear, achievable targets are established. They see the benefits of changing, and become involved in the process. This may involve attendance at, for example, drug counselling services.

- **maintenance** is that stage of the process at which the changes are consolidated. This may require ongoing attendance for specialist counselling, as well as support from other agreed sources. Parents should be alerted to the dangers of relapse, and supported if or when difficulties occur.

- **relapse** recognises that few people are able to maintain significant changes at the first attempt. Some families will relapse and exit the cycle of change, reverting to previous behaviours and positions. However, some families will re-enter the cycle and successfully learn to manage the changes to the extent that they will exit the cycle and continue to maintain the necessary changes.

The assessment should analyse the parents within the context of their capacity to change, using the following checklist.

- Does the person acknowledge the areas of concern?
- Does the person accept responsibility for the part they have played in causing those concerns?
- Does the person recognise the need to change? If not, why?
- What capacity does the person have to change?
- What desire/commitment does the person have to change?
- Is the person's partner supportive of the changes?
- Is the partner able to offer positive assistance with the changes?
- Are there systems and services available to enable change to occur?
- Are there systems and services available to support the maintenance of any changes made?
- Is the person able to make changes within a time-scale which will serve the best interests of the child(ren), accepting that delay may be prejudicial to the best interests of the child(ren)?
- Is the person able to make sufficient change within an appropriate time-scale to be able to continue to play an important part in the life of the child?

Checklist for support systems and networks

Information has been collected throughout the assessment about relationships, actions and interactions between the family and different potential systems of support, and these need to be analysed:

- Does the family have support from within the extended family?
- Describe the value, effectiveness and reliability of that support.
- Is the family likely to accept that support?
- Are there neighbours or friends who are able and prepared to offer support?
- Describe the value, effectiveness and reliability of that support.
- Is the family likely to accept that support?
- Are there any statutory or voluntary arrangements available to support agreed plans in respect of the family?

Checklist for conclusions

The final part of the assessment is to make professional judgements about the family on the basis of the information and evaluation:

- Is the family able to provide for the care of the child(ren) in ways which would always safeguard and promote their welfare?
- What range of services are needed to ensure that support to, and monitoring of the family is appropriately achieved?
- If safe care cannot be provided, why not? Describe the risk of significant harm to which the child(ren) would be exposed if they remained at home.
- What arrangements of care will serve the best interests of the child(ren)?

CHAPTER 3

Assessment: The Case Study

3.1 THE CASE STUDY ASSESSMENT

This assessment report is written so that it can be used as part of a court statement or part of a court report.

Areas of assessment are duplicated over various sections so as to provide examples of how to complete those sections. Workers completing the assessment section of their report would not necessarily duplicate the information as is done here.

Michelle

Profile

Michelle presented as anxious and nervous during most of the assessment sessions. She constantly asked for feedback and needed reassurance on a regular basis.

She co-operated extremely well with the individual sessions, although during the joint sessions she tended to be influenced by John's attitude and sometimes presented as sullen.

Michelle found many of the sessions difficult. In particular, she became upset when discussing her family and distressed when talking about the death of her grandmother and the removal of David from her care.

An educational psychology report on Michelle, prepared when she was twelve years old, concluded that:

> whilst she is academically just above the level of learning disability, social and environmental factors and a poor family life support the application for her to be placed in a Special School setting.

Michelle commented at the beginning of the assessment that her reading and writing skills were not good. Therefore, sessions were conducted using limited language. Checks were made regularly with Michelle to ensure that she understood the issues being discussed. No written material was presented to her and the checklists were all applied verbally.

Michelle's overall presentation was exclusively within the **passive** range of behaviour. The only exception to this behaviour was seen when joint interviews were conducted with John and she presented as sometimes **stubborn**. However, this behaviour was associated with John's influence and she quickly reverted to passive when not in his company.

There was no evidence of assertive, aggressive or dominant behaviour, even when Michelle disagreed with issues or events.

She demonstrated aspects of **compliant** behaviour and this was seen in her willingness to please and the extent to which she was prepared to inconvenience herself for the convenience of those around her.

She resorted to **passive/submissive** in response to pressure or criticism from John, and this will be her response when faced with personal and interpersonal conflict or situations where she is exposed to more powerful or determined characters.

These aspects of **passive/submissive** behaviour were supported by the application of a checklist designed to look at this issue.

Michelle's response to threat or perceived threat is to become **emotionally withdrawn** and **compliant**. She makes no attempt to defend herself.

This pattern of behaviour means that Michelle is vulnerable to exploitation and is therefore likely to be a **victim** to people who do not have her best interests at heart. She does not assert herself, even when that is appropriate.

Her level of passivity also means that she will not protect children she is caring for from exploitation by others.

The stubborn aspect is behaviour she has learned to present when in John's company, because it is what he expects of her. It is not a behaviour which she is likely to present in any other setting.

Michelle presents as being **emotionally fragile** and this was seen throughout the assessment. She is vulnerable to hurt and upset. Her descriptions and responses are those of a person who is easily and quickly overwhelmed by events and occurrences. She frequently 'gives in', adopting little resistance. She is therefore unlikely to be able to sustain a determined approach to issues or people.

Michelle has not been seen by a psychiatrist or psychologist in her adult life.

A self-esteem checklist was completed with Michelle and she demonstrates low self-esteem and poor self-image. This was confirmed by observation throughout the assessment.

There were times during the assessment when Michelle struggled to manage looking after herself adequately. Her level of competence is sometimes not good, especially when her self-esteem is particularly low.

Michelle has difficulties managing in the community. She is reliant on others to assist her and there has been a level of dependency on others throughout her life. She has never lived independently and would probably not manage well if she had to be entirely self-responsible. She describes feelings of loneliness and isolation when she is left alone in the flat and this indicates her low level of self-confidence and poor overall competence.

Michelle is likely to continue with her present lifestyle and living arrangements. She does not have the desire, determination, energy or resources to change things.

Overall:

- Michelle's passive/submissive behaviour means she is unable to protect herself from exploitation.

- She would also not be able to protect David from exploitation.

- There is evidence that she would be unable to manage herself competently in the community without support.

Experiences from childhood

Michelle was brought up by her mother and step-father, apart from a brief period when her grandmother cared for her. She described a community which did not generally provide her with support and she experienced bullying, victimisation and isolation. This would have had a negative effect on her emotional well-being.

She perceived her mother as being physically abusive to her, often without apparent reason. Issues of alcohol abuse and temper outbursts were significant. Michelle was more able to describe her mother in terms of task and function, what she did, rather than in terms of emotional feelings generated. The only positive comment was 'nice'.

She perceived her step-father as someone who shouted, sulked and was nasty. She remembers no positive aspects.

There was evidence of some positive experiences with the maternal grandmother and Michelle speaks fondly about her.

Michelle's relationship with her brother does not appear to have provided her with significant support. It seems to have been typically sibling.

Michelle is currently alienated from her mother and step-father and has no particular connection to her brother.

The death of her grandmother had a significant impact on her. This and other comments indicate the importance of this relationship to Michelle.

There is evidence that Michelle grew up in an environment where she experienced poor levels of parenting. She was not cared for, cared about or nurtured in ways which would allow her to grow up in an emotionally healthy manner. She was not comforted or cuddled appropriately and it is probable that her emotional well-being was not always safeguarded and promoted.

She does not appear to have been emotionally connected to either her mother or step-father. She indicates a lack of love, care, affection and attention. There was little concern for her or concern about her. There is no evidence that she was securely attached to either of them.

Michelle was physically abused by both her mother and stepfather.

She has clear memories of her parents' violence towards each other, and how fearful that made her feel. Children who grow up in a climate of such violence have their emotional well-being adversely affected. They also develop a concept of adult relationships which is distorted and learn nothing helpful or positive about the role of parents.

Experiences at school and with her grandmother are likely to have been more helpful and positive.

Michelle's parents are unlikely to have collaborated over her care and seem to have been more concerned with their own needs than hers.

Their parenting style included physical abuse, consistently negative behaviour-management strategies and little apparent interest in her welfare. There is no evidence from Michelle's report of positive management of her behaviour, or of promotion of her healthy physical and emotional development. Michelle's only positive experiences are likely to have come from her grandmother.

Michelle's perception that her parents were 'good' is idealised and her report indicates a truer understanding of the negative aspects of her childhood experiences.

She does not see herself as providing the same regime of care as her parents because she does not agree with children being smacked, and recognises the effect on children when their parents are violent to each other. There is evidence that she does not physically chastise David. Although she is not the instigator of violence, her relationship with John does have a violent aspect and David does therefore witness this.

Overall:

- Michelle's childhood experiences were not helpful to her, and her physical and emotional well-being was not properly safeguarded and promoted.

John

Profile

John is angry about the current state of affairs and made this clear throughout the assessment. Despite this, he did co-operate in the majority of the sessions. There were several areas where he refused to provide information, specifically on sources of income, and when asked about his most violent act. Whilst this is a cause of some concern, it did not affect the outcome of the assessment.

None of the sessions caused John particular upset. He did become angry from time to time, and his language and posture were frequently threatening.

John co-operated reasonably with most of the sessions and it is felt he presented his views honestly. There was a feeling that he wanted to be in control of the sessions and became frustrated and sometimes angry when he was unable to achieve this.

His refusal to co-operate, as seen in the previous assessment, was not evident this time. John was unable to give reasons for this and no reasons were apparent.

No special arrangements were necessary for the sessions.

There is no previous contact with psychological or psychiatric services.

There is no evidence of difficulties with learning and John presented within the normal range of competence. He indicated an understanding of the questions asked and material used.

John presented within the **assertive/hostile** range of behaviour, tending towards the hostile end of the range. He generally perceived all issues and interactions as a threat or potential threat and this formed the basis of his responses.

There was evidence that he uses **aggression** as a first response. It is likely that he sees any behaviour which does not present him in a powerful or determined fashion as a sign of weakness and something to be avoided at all costs.

He also sees **aggression** as his preferred response, feeling that people see him as someone who can look after himself, and this earns him respect from those with whom he generally comes into contact.

There is evidence that John would use physical violence without constraint if it suited his purpose to do so. He sees it as a legitimate part of his dealings with others. He makes no distinction between friends or strangers, men or women.

He has three convictions for offences of violence. In each case he sees his actions as appropriate and **projects** responsibility for his violence onto his victim. This inappropriate use of **projection** was also apparent when he blamed Dianne for the child protection concerns regarding Aimee.

There was an absence of any behaviour within the **passive** range, even when issues were being discussed which were non-threatening. His relationship with Michelle does not include any aspects of passive behaviour.

John seeks to establish a **dominant** position in his interactions with others and this will also be the case with relationships. He uses behaviours within the range from direct threat to subtle manipulation in order to achieve this. Dominating others is a significant aspect of John's behaviour and is clearly important to him.

Aspects of **dominance** were confirmed by a checklist designed to look at this issue.

John has dependency problems with alcohol and drugs and much of his time is taken up with acquiring money to obtain these. His use of alcohol and drugs appears to be restricted only by the extent to which he has access to them.

He is a persistent rather than chaotic user of both. He does not accept that he has a problem and feels he could stop if he wanted. I do not believe that to be the case. Withdrawing from drugs and alcohol is notoriously difficult, even with specialist help and support, and John has neither. Nor is he indicating that he would use such services as part of any programme to stop.

Drug and alcohol abuse dominates John's lifestyle and his living pattern. His routine is to acquire money to obtain drink or drugs, which he then uses until they have run out and the cycle is repeated. His personal contacts and relationship group are entirely within the drug subculture. His only known relationship with a non-abuser is with Michelle.

John's focus on satisfying his own needs is significant, and the choices he makes and actions he takes are almost always informed by that. There was no evidence in the assessment that he would ever place the needs of anyone else before his own. Further, he has little or no concern that other people might be distressed or hurt by his actions.

John's responses to the checklists involving angry and violent behaviour indicated someone who uses violence as a mechanism to get his own way, get his revenge on others, and dominate people and situations. He does not generally make any attempt to control his behaviour. He sees his angry/violent episodes as not his responsibility, but the responsibility of others who cause him to be angry/violent. He intends to continue behaving in this way in the future.

Using a checklist which looks at self-esteem, John scored within the good self-esteem range.

John manages himself in the community without external support systems and would generally reject the notion that support systems would be of any value to him. They indicate a weakness/dependence and this is something which John does not see himself as having.

His lifestyle will probably continue in the future because that is what he wants to happen. Changes will be based upon his decisions rather than anyone else's impositions. He will resist any pressure to change, and attempts to impose solutions will be met with significant resistance.

Overall:

- John's profile and behaviour cause significant concerns. His aggressive nature and violent disposition have a destructive impact on the physical and emotional well-being of all those around him.

- His determination to satisfy his own needs in disregard for the needs of others, or at the expense of others, means that those around him are likely to have their physical and emotional well-being adversely affected.

- John's unfettered use of physical violence leaves Michelle and David at risk of physical harm.

Experiences from childhood

John's childhood was spent in local authority care. He had a number of different arrangements for his care and this would lead to a lack of consistency in all aspects of his physical and emotional care.

John's periods in residential care limited his experiences of 'conventional' family life.

There is evidence that the foster placement between six and eleven years was a more positive experience for him. It is likely that he was significantly affected by the death of the foster mother and his subsequent difficult behaviour probably resulted directly from this loss.

There is evidence that John's childhood was characterised by feelings of anger, powerlessness, rejection, isolation and a lack of any control over the decisions made about him. The anger remains and he has compensated for the other aspects by adopting strategies of power in respect of, and personal control over, all aspects of his life.

John has no memory of either parent and has not met them.

He has a concept of parents which is likely to be confused by his different experiences.

His determination to get David to be tough and stand on his own feet is based upon his view that children have to bring themselves up. He has no experience of being parented, of being cared for, cared about, loved or protected by adults who would take responsibility for him. The positive experiences he may have had, between the ages of six to eleven years, have been submerged by predominantly negative experiences.

There is evidence of some emotional connection to the foster carers who looked after John for five years up to the age of eleven, but he does not appear to have been securely attached to anyone during his childhood.

Overall:

- John's childhood experiences were extremely negative.

- His current behaviour is clearly influenced by these experiences. His personal behaviour is a reaction to the lack of control he had over the events of his childhood.

- There is no evidence that any of the events of his childhood have been satisfactorily resolved.

- His strategies for child care include the use of physical punishment.

- He has a complete misunderstanding of the role and responsibility of parents in the care and management of children as they grow up.

Parenting skills and abilities

Michelle

Michelle has some understanding of the basic physical needs of a child, in particular a child's need for food, shelter and warmth. She is also sufficiently aware of issues of safety.

She understands a child's need for love, care and attention and the need for a child to be raised in an environment where the child's emotional and developmental needs will be safeguarded and promoted.

Her ability to provide for a child's physical, emotional and developmental needs is limited by her ability to exercise parental authority and the way in which her passive/submissive behaviour prevents her from being able to safeguard the child from exploitation by others. This exploitation could involve significant harm. In addition there is evidence that David exploits his mother's vulnerability.

Michelle has a positive image of David. Their relationship is characterised by positive engagement when David is doing what he wants, and conflict when he is prevented from doing so or when Michelle is unable to satisfy his needs immediately. In this respect, David is in control of the relationship. Michelle's behaviour indicates acceptance of this. She will accommodate whatever David wants because she is unable to manage his behaviour when he tantrums. David is aware of this and uses it to his advantage.

There is evidence that Michelle loves her son and she has an emotional connection to him.

Michelle's ability to provide a consistent, stable environment for David is affected by her poor self-esteem, her dependence on John and her inability to manage David's challenging behaviour when he is with her.

She struggles to provide for David's safe physical care because she cannot protect him from others, and her own emotional well-being is frequently so low that she has difficulty managing her own needs.

Michelle is not able to use parental authority effectively and this means that there are times when David is effectively out of her control. At other times he dominates his mother to an extent that he is learning that he can do what he wants when he wants.

There is an emotional connection between Michelle and David which is seen in the generally positive image she has of him and the genuine affection she shows towards him. She does not, however, always comfort David in positive ways. She sees him as being like his father (and that is a negative indicator) and she does not use discipline appropriately. David does not respond appropriately to his mother, keep himself occupied in positive ways, respond to parental limit-setting, or always react appropriately to physical closeness. It is therefore likely that there is not a secure attachment between David and his mother.

Michelle does not use distraction, diversion, negotiation or compromise in respect of David's behaviour. Nor does she use parental authority. She is reactive to David rather than being proactive in engagement with him. There are significant difficulties with her child care management strategies and this is evident in the fact that David is clearly in charge of their relationship.

Michelle finds parenting David difficult and this was confirmed by a checklist designed to look at parental stress.

Michelle's response to the injury to David was appropriate. However, her poor levels of competence and poor self-esteem are likely to see her overwhelmed by the need to respond appropriately at all times to sudden emergencies.

Michelle's overall skills to parent are not always good enough. She is unable to establish a position with David which makes it clear that she is the parent and he is the child; that she is in charge, and that she can exercise parental authority appropriately. She allows David to prioritise their needs for them.

She cannot ensure David's safety because she is unable to safeguard him from exploitation by other people.

Her own personal resources are often exhausted by the energy required to look after herself, and she has nothing in reserve to care for David.

John

John's understanding of the physical, emotional and developmental needs of a child is confined to a perception that children should be taught to fend for themselves as soon as possible and thereafter left to get on with that process.

He sees his parenting responsibility as being to make children as tough as possible, as soon as possible.

He had some previous parenting experience whilst he lived with Dianne A although this was limited. Fartown social services department record their involvement with the family as resulting from allegations of domestic violence. They were also concerned about John's attitude to discipline.

He sees the parenting role as one which is designed to keep children in their place and his concept is that children should be 'seen and not heard'. He expects immediate compliance and obedience from David. John perceives David in exclusively negative terms.

His relationship is based on the presumption that David will do what he is told when he is told, and that is evident in all of the interactions between them. John reinforces that state of affairs at every opportunity.

He perceives his role as that of secondary carer and does not commit himself to any primary care responsibilities.

John does not use parental authority appropriately, he uses it absolutely. John conceded that in the past he has reinforced this with physical chastisement, but now he merely has to give David 'one of his looks'. David's immediate compliance, the descriptions given by himself and Michelle and the 'frozen awareness' seen at the hospital, all indicate that David is terrified of John. This will inevitably lead to David suffering significant harm.

There is no evidence of any emotional connection or attachment between David and John, and John's attitude and behaviour would support this.

John's management strategies are based upon force and fear. There are no elements of compromise, negotiation, accommodation, distraction or discussion. There was also no evidence of positive reinforcement of good behaviour, but considerable evidence of negative sanctions for what he considered to be bad behaviour. John's concept of bad behaviour would be considered as being within normal limits for many active, growing children. For example, John sees 'not doing as they are told' as naughty behaviour worthy of a smack.

John does not find parenting at all stressful because he does not allow himself to become emotionally engaged in the parenting process, or physically involved, except in a superficial way when it suits him.

David's extremely compliant behaviour is his response to the power and control which John exercises over him.

John does not prioritise David's needs over his own needs, nor is he likely to do so in the future. He does not have the physical or emotional resources to parent David. He uses his resources to exercise power, control and dominance, and to show rejection.

Combined parenting

The parenting styles of Michelle and John are at opposite ends of the spectrum and in no way complementary to each other. Michelle's inability to assert any control over David, and John's absolute control, will leave David dominating one and being submissive to the other. He is likely to internalise that in an unhelpful manner at some time in the future.

Neither parenting style ensures David's physical or emotional safety, and both are likely to lead to significant physical and emotional harm.

The impact of alcohol and drug abuse on parenting

Michelle does not abuse alcohol or drugs, and the issue of joint intoxication does not therefore arise.

However, she is not able to ensure David's safety when John is intoxicated, because of her submissive behaviour to John.

The priority for family finances is to keep John supplied with drugs and alcohol, and David's needs are of secondary importance.

There is no significant difference in the quality of care provided when John is intoxicated. David has a pattern of being difficult and demanding when his mother is looking after him, and passive when John is around. David is not yet of an age where he is able to distinguish whether John is or is not able to exercise parental control. However, that time will eventually come if the family is reunited, and this will create a new set of dynamics.

There are ongoing concerns that John is not sufficiently diligent in ensuring that his drug equipment is kept safe. John's friends are frequent visitors and Michelle has confirmed that they inject in the flat. David is exposed to this and will become familiar with the drug subculture. This is likely to make him less resistant to the use of drugs as he gets older. Additionally, intoxicated adults may behave in ways which risk causing significant harm to children.

The abuse of drugs and alcohol dominates the activities, lifestyle and daily routines within the house. All aspects of living within the drug subculture are embraced.

The individual and collective parenting styles of Michelle and John place David at risk of physical injury and emotional harm.

There is already evidence of physical injury to David whilst in their care.

Relationship between Michelle and John

Michelle and John have been together for approximately eight months. Their relationship presents as settled and stable. Each has an understanding of their role within the relationship and appears 'content' with it.

The relationship between them is one within which John is entirely dominant and Michelle is completely submissive.

John comes and goes as he likes and he expects Michelle to be there to respond appropriately to his needs and demands. He enforces and reinforces his control over Michelle by hitting her when she does not respond within his imposed time-scale to his needs and demands.

From John's point of view the arrangement is entirely satisfactory. He uses Michelle's income to supplement his own, he comes and goes as he wants, and Michelle is waiting for him when he comes home. His list of statements about their relationship indicates a high priority on autonomy, freedom and personal space, and a low priority on an emotional connection to her.

Michelle sees the relationship as something which affords her some protection from others. John will not let other people take advantage of Michelle. She has limited self-sufficiency skills and depends on others to provide her with support. She would rather be with someone than be on her own and has reported that being alone frightens her. The cost to her for those benefits within her present relationship is to be physically and emotionally abused by John and to be exploited by him. It is a price she is clearly willing to pay, and as things are she is unlikely to exit the relationship.

John's view is that he will not allow Michelle to exit the relationship unless that is his choice.

The relationship is characterised by violence. It is not a partnership, but one in which John exercises all the power.

David will witness physical and emotional abuse and that will have a significant impact on him. He will learn nothing about 'normal' adult relationships in which care, concern, giving, reciprocation, partnership, collaboration, mutual respect and joint parenting arrangements should feature. Nor will he benefit from any of those arrangements or the positive experiences they would provide for him.

Health

Michelle has no significant health issues.

John is a long-term alcohol and drug abuser. He is beginning to show the typical signs of 'wear and tear' associated with that. He is currently under investigation for circulation problems and it is likely that he will not be well in the long term.

Criminal history

Michelle has no criminal history.

John has convictions as a juvenile which are not relevant, and for drug-related offences and violence as an adult.

His breach of order offences indicate a determination on his part not to co-operate unless that is his choice, and his refusal to accept imposition. His comment 'no one tells me what to do' has an implication for his ability to make changes.

The offences involving drugs are of concern because they are likely to have involved people visiting to buy and sell drugs, and involvement in the drug subculture. Drug-related activities are known to involve dispute and violence. Intoxicated people are likely to visit and are capable of dangerous behaviour. Lifestyles and daily routines are dominated by drugs. Children who are living in this environment are at risk of physical injury. Their healthy development is unlikely to be a priority for the parents and they are therefore likely to suffer significant harm.

John's violent offences are of particular concern. They demonstrate his capacity to use violence when he chooses and to project the blame for that onto the victims. The offence where he waited for the opportunity to assault a female who had shown him up demonstrates his capacity for violence which is prompted not by sudden loss of temper or control, but by aspects of premeditation.

Discussion with John about his violent offences and his attitude to the use of violence indicate that it is an incorporated part of his behaviour and responses, and is therefore likely to be used as and when necessary in the future. This is a significantly negative indicator.

Finances

There is evidence that the financial priorities are to keep John supplied with drugs and alcohol and that all other financial commitments are of secondary importance. Debts currently include rent and electricity, and both of these are relevant to the proper care of David as they have an impact on shelter, food and warmth.

David

David is a 4-year-old, white male child. He lived with his mother until his recent accommodation by the local authority. For the first three years he was looked after by his mother and her grandmother. During the last eight months he has been looked after by his mother and John.

He has in the past presented as an active little boy whom the nursery found to be behaving within normal limits.

There is evidence that his mother has had increasing difficulty in managing David and he had begun to dominate their relationship. He has presented his mother with difficult and demanding behaviour which has appeared to overwhelm her and she has resorted to giving in to him. He is in control of his behaviour, even when in apparent tantrum, and it is therefore a manipulation technique he has successfully developed.

When David is in the company of John he presents as a withdrawn little boy. He remains still for long periods apart from some occasional 'body rocking'. He is immediately responsive to John's requests and demands. There is no evidence of demanding behaviour. He avoids close proximity to John and when this is necessary he flinches in response to any sudden movements. His behaviour is within the passive/submissive range. David presents significant behaviour which indicates he is extremely fearful of John.

Since being with foster carers, the appropriate use of parental authority is having an impact and David is beginning to use more acceptable behaviours. He still has tantrums but their duration and severity is reducing. He is beginning to realise that he does not achieve his intended purpose through tantrum. He does not approach the foster carers for hugs or comfort, but he is beginning to accept affection when it is offered. He will not go to sleep without a light on and has nightmares several times each week. These include 'men coming to get him', and 'people coming into his room and scaring him'. When he wakes from a nightmare he has to be comforted for considerable periods of time.

Before contact with his mother and John, David becomes anxious and withdrawn, and this continues until after the contact is over. He has been physically sick several times before contact and he has also soiled his bed on some nights before contact.

David presents within the normal range of physical development and this has been confirmed by the recent medical examination. His speech is also within normal limits, although his vocabulary is poor and this may indicate a lack of stimulation in this area. There is evidence that for long periods David has been left to play alone and entertain himself and this would seem to confirm this issue of stimulation. There were few age-appropriate toys evident.

David's immunisations are up to date.

During the period immediately preceding the injury to David, poor conditions in the flat were identified. David's bedding was inadequate.

David's daily routines were not consistent. He has been observed in bed during the early afternoon and still up during the late evening.

David's emotional well-being has been affected by the very different parenting styles of his mother and John.

The emotional climate in the home is not good. The relationship between Michelle and John is characterised by violence. Michelle adopts the same passive/compliant behaviour as her son David when in the presence of John. John is known to become angry quite often. When he is drunk or on drugs his behaviour could be dangerous and unpredictable. Levels of anxiety, fear and uncertainty prevail, and these help to create an emotionally poor climate.

David's behaviour with his mother and John is of concern. With Michelle he has a relationship where he has the power, and has developed extreme behaviours which enforce and reinforce this. With John he is compliant to an extent which is unhelpful to his healthy emotional development.

There are few positive connections with either his mother or John, and many worrying features.

During the final period at home David's self-esteem will have been poor. Whilst it is still not good, there are signs of improvement. For example, he is beginning to take pride in achievements and he accepts praise and positive reinforcement now.

Significant harm

David suffered physical injuries, including bone fractures which expert medical opinion concluded were caused non-accidentally. The medical report refers to significant force being used. These injuries occurred whilst he was being looked after by his mother and John. Although it has not been possible to identify the perpetrator, it must be concluded that either Michelle or John, either solely or together, injured him, or that David was injured whilst in their care and they failed to protect him from that significant harm. They either committed the injuries or failed to protect him from receiving the injuries.

John has admitted physically chastising David.

David lived in an environment where domestic violence was prevalent. Children who live in such a home environment are at risk of physical injury during a violent episode between the adults. The emotional impact on them of living in an environment where fear, anger, animosity, resentment, dispute and violent dispute occur is significant.

Significant drug and/or alcohol abuse were present and David was at risk of accidentally ingesting potentially harmful substances. He was also at risk of physical injury from needles and the paraphernalia of drug-taking.

Intoxicated adults placed David at risk from their actions and were unable to ensure his protection from dangerous or unsafe situations.

The conflicting and contradictory child management systems are likely to have left David confused and uncertain. John's aggressive parenting style has left David anxious, fearful and traumatised. His 'frozen awareness', the behaviour and responses before contact, his passive/submissive behaviour, and the 'flinching' when in proximity to John are all evidence of this. David has therefore suffered significant emotional harm whilst he was living at home.

Capacity for change

Michelle recognises that she has some difficulty in managing David. She does not see that the care of David was unacceptable, nor does she accept that David has been injured non-accidentally. Michelle does not think there is a problem, because John can manage David's behaviour.

She does not believe that they need to change things before David is returned to them.

John intends to continue to use drugs and alcohol. He does not intend to make any changes in his lifestyle, nor does he feel that any changes are necessary. He sees himself as a competent parent whose child management strategies are good and positive. He believes his concept of parenting is appropriate.

Neither Michelle nor John accepts the concerns expressed about the care of David.

It is therefore clear that Michelle and John do not have any of the essential prerequisites for change, an acknowledgement of concerns, accepting responsibility for concerns, or recognising the need for change. Without these, the process of change will not be engaged.

Support systems

Michelle and John do not have any support systems from within the family.

Friends are all part of the drug and alcohol subculture and therefore they are not likely to offer any purposeful support.

Conclusion

Michelle and John are not able to look after David in ways which will safeguard and promote his welfare.

Michelle is the only person with parental responsibility and she is unable to look after him safely as a sole carer.

David has already suffered physical injuries and emotional harm. If he were returned to the care of his mother and John he would be at immediate risk of significant physical and emotional harm.

Michelle and John do not want to change. Even if they did and even if such change were possible, it could not be achieved within a time-scale that would serve David's best interests.

3.2 POSITIVE OUTCOMES FROM ASSESSMENT

The case study concludes that David cannot be safely returned to his mother and her partner or be placed within the family. However, there will be assessments which do conclude that such placements can be made and that the risk of significant harm has either been removed or can be appropriately managed.

The Children Act 1989, Section 17 (local authority support for children and families) identifies a clear responsibility to promote the upbringing of children by their families, where that can be achieved in ways which safeguard and promote the welfare of the child.

Workers will no doubt assess families where the parents are unable to provide for the safe care of their child but where there are, for example, grandparents, aunts, uncles, cousins or nieces who are both prepared to and capable to look after the child. Where there is a possibility of such placements being made, the adults involved should be assessed, using all of the guidelines and checklists contained within this book.

Placement with relatives

There are specific advantages for a child being brought up within the family:

- The parents can continue to play a significant role in the lives of the child.

- Existing relationships which have a positive impact on the emotional well-being of the child can be maintained.

- Positive attachments, including aspects of secure attachment to relatives, can be maintained.

- Contact with parents is maintained on a 'natural' basis as part of the day-to-day living arrangements for the family.

- The child is brought up with a knowledge and understanding of the birth parents, and has the opportunity to engage and interact with them.

- Cultural, ethnic, religious, subcultural and community links are maintained for the child.

- Extended family relationships are maintained.

There are however, considerations which must be made as part of any assessment of family members, and which should be balanced against the advantages:

- Relationships between family members are sometimes difficult, and this can have an impact on the care which can be provided.

- Parents can resent the placement of their child with a family member, and the potential for them to disrupt the placement should be assessed.

- Disagreements can arise over the care arrangements, and this can affect relationships within the family.

- The relative carers may not present the child with a positive image of one or both of the parents.

- If relationships between the parents and relative carers become strained or alienated, the child may be faced with having to make choices or will have divided loyalties, which would have an impact on his/her emotional well-being.

- Family relationships may become distorted. For example, a child who is being cared for by a grandparent may begin to see that adult as their parent, and the parent then may be perceived as a sibling.

The placement of a child with members of the birth family could be made under The Foster Placement (Children) Regulations 1991, if s/he is being looked after with the consent of his/her mother under Section 20, Children Act 1989, or subject to a care order, Section 31, Children Act 1989.

Immediate placements with relatives can be made under Regulation 11, The Foster Placement Regulations 1991, prior to the full assessment of the extended family members for suitability as foster-carers. In these circumstances essential checks with the police, child protection agencies, education and health authorities would be made before the immediate placement is made.

Placement with parents

There are circumstances where the local authority has intervened to protect a child and where the subsequent assessment concludes that it is possible for the child to be returned home and looked after in ways which would safeguard and promote the welfare of the child.

Issues which would be significant in concluding that the child can return home would include:

- a thorough understanding of the significant harm, or risk of significant harm, including where appropriate the perpetrator(s) of injuries or harm

- a child care environment in which the child will be protected from significant harm or the risk of significant harm

- an attachment to the parent(s) which includes aspects of secure attachment, or agreed work designed to achieve secure attachments

- a child protection plan which safeguards and promotes the welfare of the child and provides appropriate support and monitoring

- the use of family, child protection services and services for children and families, to support the parent(s)

- mechanisms to improve the skills and abilities of the parent(s), for example, parenting skills

- strategies to support the child appropriately whilst new skills are being developed

- appropriate counselling to deal with life experiences – for example, abusive experiences in childhood – which are having an impact on the physical or emotional well-being of the parent, and therefore having an impact on their ability to look after the child safely.

Children who are returned to the care of their parents in cases where no court order is in force, are usually subject to a child protection plan which informs the placement.

If the child is subject to a care order, any return to parent(s) has to comply with The Placement of Children with Parents etc. Regulations 1991.

3.3 CONCLUSION

Assessing parents in matters of child protection is a complex and intriguing task. It requires levels of skill which should be underpinned by professional training and informed by ongoing training and professional development.

In the early years, workers were not well prepared for the responsibilities heaped on them by a society which became increasingly aware of the extent to which children were being ill-treated and neglected, and abused in ways which were not even imagined.

Enquiries and reports, research and good practice identified the failings in child protection systems and exposed the weaknesses in practice. Macro-systems were designed by government, government departments, regional services and local authorities, and these provided a basis from which policy and procedure could be, and were, developed. In order to keep pace with the macro-systems which were being introduced, practitioners needed to 'catch up' with the enormous progress being made in the identification, assessment and management of child protection matters. Milestone events, such as the publication of *Protecting Children: A Guide for Social Workers Undertaking a Comprehensive Assessment* (DoH 1988) laid the foundations for the assessment of individual families. Publications have brought increased knowledge, understanding and grasp to the subject, along with solutions, innovations and guidance. Research, literature and education have provided the information and a statistical evidence-base to support the assessment and decision-making processes. Most recently the *Framework for the Assessment of Children in Need and their Families* (DoH 2000) has added enormously to the information base for assessment work.

This tool has focused on the assessment of parents within the child protection spectrum. It relies mainly on the practical experience of those who work on a day-to-day basis with the dangerous, demanding, troubled and troublesome families who have harmed their children or placed them at risk of significant harm.

It is hoped that practitioners using this manual will find the training material of great benefit and assistance in their future work in child protection when undertaking the assessment of parents. It is also hoped that those professionals who provide a training service in child protection will find this training manual a valuable resource of additional material, information and exercises.

A Guide to the Children Act 1989

It is important for workers to know how current child care legislation informs, underpins and supports the work of child protection. This section does not aim to provide a detailed analysis of the Act, but refers workers to those parts which are significant to practice.

The Children Act 1989 consolidated all previous legislation so that care proceedings can now only be pursued through this Act.

The Adoption Act 1976 remains in force and deals with issues of freeing for adoption, and adoption.

Significantly, private law (applications stemming from divorce, separation and family disputes) was incorporated into the Act along with public law matters (care and adoption).

The following sections of the Children Act 1989 are relevant to child protection matters.

WELFARE OF THE CHILD – SECTION 1

This section introduces the concept that the child's welfare is the paramount consideration, and in Subsection 3 lists the issues about which the court shall have regard. Subsection 3 is referred to as 'the welfare checklist'.

Statements which are provided in court proceedings, the report of the 'children's guardian' (formerly guardian ad litem) and assessment reports frequently use the welfare checklist. It provides a focus on those areas which are vital to the decision-making process. Workers using the checklist are unlikely to omit important information.

1. (1) When a court determines any question with respect to –

   (a) the upbringing of a child; or

   (b) the administration of a child's property or the application of any income arising from it;

   the child's welfare shall be the court's paramount consideration.

(2)   In any proceedings in which any question with respect to the upbringing of a child arises, the court shall have regard to the general principle that any delay in determining the question is likely to prejudice the welfare of the child.

(3)   In the circumstances mentioned in subsection (4), a court shall have regard in particular to –

    (a) the ascertainable wishes and feelings of the child concerned (considered in the light of his age and understanding);

    (b) his physical, emotional and educational needs;

    (c) the likely effect on him of any change in his circumstances;

    (d) his age, sex, background and any characteristics of his which the court considers relevant;

    (e) any harm which he has suffered or is at risk of suffering;

    (f) how capable each of his parents, and any other person in relation to whom the court considers the question to be relevant, is of meeting his needs;

    (g) the range of powers available to the court under this Act in the proceedings in question.

(4)   The circumstances are that –

    (a) the court is considering whether to make, vary or discharge a section 8 order (note 1), and the making, variation or discharge of the order is opposed by any party to the proceedings; or

    (b) the court is considering whether to make, vary or discharge an order under Part IV.

(5)   If the court is considering whether or not to make one or more orders under this Act with respect to a child, it shall not make the order or any of the orders unless it considers that doing so would be better for the child than making no order at all.

Note 1. Section 8 orders address issues of residence, contact, (private law) specific issues and prohibited steps. If the court makes a residence order, the person in whose favour that order is made acquires 'parental responsibility'. Parental responsibility comprises the legal rights and duties in respect of the child, except for the right to consent to the making of an adoption order, the right to change the child's name, or to give consent to the child emigrating. The birth mother automatically has parental responsibility, as does any birth father who is married to or marries the birth mother. In other circumstances, parental responsibility can be acquired by way of agreement, or by court order.

CARE AND SUPERVISION ORDERS – SECTION 31

Care and supervision orders would usually only be made in care proceedings where a full assessment had been made of the needs of the children, including the ability of the parents to safeguard and promote their welfare.

The court can only make an order when to do so is better than making no order at all. This is referred to as the 'no order principle' and is contained in Section 1(5) of the Act.

Supervision orders are usually considered by the court in circumstances where children are living at home and where the court considers that the statutory involvement of the local authority is necessary to safeguard and promote the welfare of the child. A Supervision Order empowers the local authority to visit the family, provide support and monitor issues of child care and child protection.

Care orders are considered by the court if it is expected that the child will be looked after away from the family home, by the local authority, although in exceptional circumstances children are looked after at home immediately a care order is made. When a care order is made, the local authority acquires parental responsibility, which it shares with any other person with parental responsibility (usually the parents).

Local authorities are required to work in partnership with parents and other people with parental responsibility, although they do have the power to determine the extent to which a parent or guardian of the child may meet his/her parental responsibility. In this, the local authority's parental responsibility is 'superior'.

Applications for care and supervision orders are made in the following circumstances.

31. (2) A court may only make a Care Order or supervision order if it is satisfied –

(a) that the child concerned is suffering, or is likely to suffer, significant harm; and

(b) that the harm, or likelihood of harm, is attributable to –

(i) the care given to the child, or likely to be given to him if the order were not made, not being what it would be reasonable to expect a parent to give to him; or

(ii) the child's being beyond parental control.

CHILD ASSESSMENT ORDER – SECTION 43

Child assessment orders are usually the appropriate way forward when there are long-term cumulative concerns about the children, for example, neglect, but it is felt that the assessment can be completed whilst the children remain living at home.

It was envisaged that this order would cover that uncomfortable gap between the risk of leaving children at home and the drastic step of removing them. However, in practice it is a little used part of the legislation. The difficulty in using this order comes in trying to organise a series of examinations and assessment involving experts from different disciplines, within the same brief time-scale – for example, within the same week.

43. (1) On the application of a local authority or authorised person for an order to be made under this section with respect to a child, the court may make the order if, but only if, it is satisfied that –

   (a) the applicant has reasonable cause to suspect that the child is suffering, or is likely to suffer, significant harm;

   (b) an assessment of the state of the child's health or development, or of the way in which he has been treated, is required to enable the applicant to determine whether or not the child is suffering, or is likely to suffer, significant harm; and

   (c) it is unlikely that such an assessment will be made or be satisfactory, in the absence of an order under this section.

EMERGENCY PROTECTION ORDER – SECTION 44

Emergency protection orders (EPOs) can be made for a period of up to eight days. They should be used to offer immediate protection for a child and permit the local authority to remove the child from home for the period of the order. EPOs are usually used as the first part of the care proceedings process. They can be 'ex parte' applications, which means the applicant can go to a magistrate or judge and apply for an EPO without the parents or their legal representative being there to oppose the order being made.

44. (1) Where any person ('the applicant') applies to the court for an order to be made under this section with respect to a child, the court may make the order if, but only if, it is satisfied that –

   (a) there is reasonable cause to believe that the child is likely to suffer significant harm if –

(i) he is not removed to the accommodation provided by or on behalf of the applicant; or

(ii) he does not remain in the place in which he is then being accommodated.

REMOVAL AND ACCOMMODATION OF CHILDREN BY POLICE IN CASES OF EMERGENCY – SECTION 46

This section enables police officers to provide immediate protection for children, pending the intervention of the local authority social services department. It should be noted that this is not an order and therefore does not require the permission of the court. In practice, police officers would immediately inform the local authority social services department, who would assume the care and responsibility for the child.

46. (1) Where a constable has reasonable cause to believe that a child would otherwise be likely to suffer significant harm, he may –

   (a) remove the child to suitable accommodation and keep him there; or

   (b) take such steps as are reasonable to ensure that the child's removal from any hospital, or other place, in which he is then being accommodated is prevented.

LOCAL AUTHORITY'S DUTY TO INVESTIGATE – SECTION 47

The local authority has a duty to investigate all circumstances where it is reported to them, or they believe, that there may be child protection issues in respect of the child. Referrals of a child protection nature are investigated under this section.

47. (1) Where the Local Authority –

   (a) are informed that a child who lives, or is found, in their area

      (i) is the subject of an emergency protection order, or

      (ii) is in police protection; or

   (b) have reasonable cause to suspect that a child who lives, or is found, in their area is suffering, or is likely to suffer significant harm,

      the authority shall make, or cause to be made, such enquiries as they consider necessary to enable them to decide whether they should take any action to safeguard or promote the child's welfare.

Some Terms from Child Protection

CRITERIA FOR PLACING A CHILD'S NAME ON THE CHILD PROTECTION REGISTER

Child abuse is taken to refer to any child under the age of seventeen years who has suffered significant harm, or is likely to suffer significant harm, as the result of a direct act, or a failure to act to provide proper care, or both.

Registration usually occurs when a child protection case conference reaches the conclusion that:

- significant harm is confirmed or strongly suspected or potential significant harm is identified

and

- an inter-agency child protection plan is regarded as necessary for the welfare of the child.

The categories of registration are:

Neglect

This is the persistent or severe neglect of a child, or failure to protect a child from exposure to any kind of danger (for example, cold, starvation, being left unattended, not seeking appropriate medical attention or extreme failure to carry out important aspects of care) resulting in the significant impairment of the child's health or development, including non-organic failure to thrive.

Physical harm

This is actual or likely physical injury to a child, or failure to prevent physical injury (or suffering) to a child, including deliberate poisoning, suffocation and Munchausen syndrome by proxy.

Sexual harm

This is the actual or likely sexual exploitation of a child or adolescent. The child may be dependent and/or developmentally immature, does not truly comprehend, or is unable to give informed consent. The abuser may use bribes, threats or physical force to persuade the child or adolescent to participate in sexual activity.

Emotional harm

This is the actual, or likely, severe adverse effect on a child's emotional and behavioural development, caused by persistent or severe emotional ill-treatment or rejection. It includes persistent scapegoating, criticism, bullying, harassment, ridiculing, belittling or frightening.

All abuse involves some emotional ill-treatment. This category of registration should be used where it is the sole or main form of abuse.

Child protection case conferences

A child protection case conference is a multi-disciplinary, inter-agency forum in which information is exchanged and decisions made about the risks to children. It is the vehicle through which decisions are made as to whether or not the names of children should be placed on the child protection register. Each area has a child protection register. The purpose of the register is to provide a record of all children in the area who are currently the subjects of an inter-agency protection plan, and to ensure that the plans are formally reviewed at least every six months. The register also provides a central point of speedy enquiry for professional staff who are worried about a child and want to know whether the child is the subject of an inter-agency protection plan, or has been subject to previous enquiries or registration.

Initial child protection case conference

A conference should be convened through the child protection services in the following circumstances:

- following an investigation which indicates that an incident of abuse has occurred and/or that a decision needs to be made about safeguarding the child concerned from future abuse or the possibility of future abuse

- if a child is living in a household where a person previously involved in the abuse of a child(ren) is living or is a frequent visitor

- if it is considered that an unborn child may be subject to risk and there is a need to develop a child protection plan before the birth

- if a child who is on the child protection register in another area moves into the area concerned

- if a child or young person is subject to allegations of abuse against another child, or has been found to have abused another child

- if a child returning home from local authority care has previously been abused and the risk to the child is likely to increase.

Child protection review case conference

A child protection review case conference should take place within every six months of the initial child protection case conference, or the previous review case conference.

The review case conference provides an opportunity for an update of the family's circumstances, and to review whether or not continued registration serves the best interests of the child.

Appropriate consideration should be given to bringing child protection review case conferences forward, or convening them at short notice:

- if there is a further injury to, or a serious incident involving a child on the child protection register

- if there is a significant change of circumstances requiring changes in the child protection plan

- if there is an inability to effect recommendations of a child protection plan and this leads to increased risk to a child, or prevents what is considered to be the necessary reduction of risk.

APPENDIX: EXERCISES

EXERCISE 1 – CASE STUDY ON FAMILY STRUCTURE

Janice is a 24-year-old single mother of two children. Fiona is aged 3 and John is aged 2. Child protection workers are concerned about the poor quality of physical care being provided to the children by Janice. Allegations have been made that she leaves the children locked in the house for long periods, and neighbours report that the children frequently complain about being hungry.

The assessment session with Janice looking at her family structure provided the following information:

- Her parents are separated and the whereabouts of her father is not known. Her mother has remarried and Janice does not get on with her step-father. Janice says that her mother does not know about the present difficulties with the children and would probably not be allowed to help her because of her step-father.

- Janice has two older sisters, Clare, aged 30, and Sarah, aged 29, and a younger half-brother, Paul, is aged 12. Clare lives nearby with her partner and three children. Janice used to see Clare almost every day but has avoided her in the last few months because the house always seems to be untidy and she does not want Clare to see how difficult things are for her.

- Janice's sister Sarah has two children and currently lives alone. Her partner is serving a prison sentence for drug-related offences. Sarah is a registered heroin addict. Sarah's children are on the child protection register under the category of physical injury. Janice reported that she has not spoken to her sister since they had an argument because of Sarah's drug-taking.

- Janice's half-brother Paul lives with Janice's mother and step-father. Although Paul's father has stopped him from visiting Janice, he sneaks round at least twice a week. Janice reports that she has a good relationship with Paul and he spends a lot of time playing with Fiona and John.

- Analyse the relationships within the family.

- Could the involvement with any members of the family assist in safeguarding and promoting the welfare of the children?

- Are there any additional questions you would have asked?

- Are there any answers you would have explored further?

EXERCISE 2 – CASE STUDY ON CHRONOLOGY

❑ Paul was born in London. When he was 2 years of age his father left the family home. Paul has no memory of him and they had no subsequent contact.

❑ Paul lived with his mother until he was 8 years of age and then she met Roger J. Paul remembers that there were arguments from time to time during the first two years, but generally things were okay. After that the arguments became more violent and he has vivid memories of Roger J hitting his mother on a regular basis. On the occasions when Paul attempted to intervene he was also hit.

❑ When he was 11 years of age Paul and his mother left home and went to live in a refuge many miles away in order to escape from Roger J. Although he was pleased to have left Roger J, Paul remembers this as a sad period in his life. In particular he was separated from the friends with whom he had grown up and attended school.

❑ They lived in the hostel for approximately six months and then Paul and his mother moved into their own house. Shortly after moving in they became friendly with a neighbour, Stephen D. Stephen D spent more and more time with them and eventually he moved in. Paul remembers they all sat down and talked about whether or not this was a good idea and he was really pleased when Stephen D moved in.

❑ According to Paul, the next two years were brilliant. However, Stephen D was then killed in a road traffic accident. Paul reported that he still gets upset about this and he sometimes cries.

❑ Paul remembers that his mother then became really depressed and started to drink heavily. She had a number of boyfriends but most of them also had a problem with drink.

- □ Paul remembers that he often had to get himself ready for school and frequently there was nothing for him to have for his breakfast.

- □ One of his mother's boyfriends attempted to sexually assault him, but Paul was able to run away. He told his mother about this but she did not believe him.

- □ Eventually things became so difficult at home that Paul left and moved into a bedsit. He thinks he was about 16 years of age at the time.

- □ He then lived in a variety of bedsit accommodation until he met Marie L when he was 20 years of age.

- □ Marie L is 16 years older than Paul and people often pick on them because of this.

- Identify the positive aspects for Paul within this chronology.

- What are the events in this chronology which would have had an adverse impact on Paul's physical and emotional well-being?

- Are there likely to be any matters for Paul which remain unresolved?

- Are there aspects of Paul's chronology which would give rise to concerns?

- What issues from this chronology would need to be further investigated?

- Is there any information which is likely to impact upon Paul's ability and competence as an adult?

- Are there any issues of particular relevance to child protection?

- Is there any information which would give a clue to Paul's experiences from childhood?

- Is there any information which would be the focus of discussions when exploring Paul's experiences from childhood?

- Are there any other questions which need to be asked?

EXERCISE 3 – CASE STUDY ON EXPERIENCES FROM CHILDHOOD

Tina is 23-year-old single mother. She has a son, Carl, who is aged five and is presenting aggressive behaviour at school. The school has expressed concerns because Tina is frequently seen to lose her temper with Carl and has been seen to handle him roughly on occasions when she has collected him from school. Tina reports that she does have difficulty sometimes controlling her temper.

Tina reported the following experiences from childhood.

- ❑ She described her mother in the following terms:

    'She was okay…when she was in a good mood.'

    'There were times when she lost her temper with us.'

    'She would shout at us and belt us if we did not do what we were told.'

    'I can't remember the number of times I was sent to bed without any tea.'

    'She had a temper on her.'

    'Her and my dad used to argue all the time… They used to have fist fights out in the street.'

    'I loved her really… She died before I was able to tell her.'

Tina considered her mother's best feature was 'she was a brilliant cook' and she least liked her mother 'because she was always losing her temper with us'.

- ❑ She remembers her father worked as a milkman and consequently he was out of the house very early but always at home by the time she returned from school. She described him in the following terms:

    'He was brilliant…he would play with us whenever he could.'

    'He never really stood up to my mother when they argued.'

    'He could be a bit nasty when he had been out drinking.'

    'He always tried to provide for us.'

    'I was his favourite.'

- ❑ Tina reported that she had five younger siblings and she tended to spend a lot of time looking after them, especially at night when her parents went to the pub.

- Tina remembers being cuddled by her father from time to time, but never by her mother. She always felt that after she had been cuddled by her father, her mother would find fault with something she was doing or saying and punish her.

- She recognises that her father spoiled her and never punished her, even when she was naughty.

- Tina and her siblings were frequently smacked by their mother and Tina feels that she was always hit harder than the other children, and that there were occasions when she was smacked for things she had not done. She commented that her mother would always believe her younger brothers and sisters and frequently accused her of lying.

- When she was thirteen year of age, Tina was sexually assaulted by her maternal grandfather. She told her mother immediately but was accused of being a liar. After that she felt that her mother punished her even more than she had previously.

- When Tina was fifteen years of age, her mother died suddenly. Tina reported feelings of relief, fear, anger and distress. She felt that she had to keep these feelings inside her because she had to look after the young children. Her father stopped work but he provided little assistance because he was devastated at the loss of his wife. He started to suffer from bouts of depression, and even now he has periods when he has to be admitted to psychiatric hospital.

- Tina found it extremely difficult looking after her younger siblings. She was expected to get them ready for school, prepare all the meals, do all the shopping, washing and housework. As a result of this she did not attend school for most of her last year.

- Eventually Tina left home following an argument with her father because she felt he was not doing enough to help.

- She remembers the following good things from her childhood:
  - playing with dad
  - staying on her uncle's farm when she was small.

- She remembers the following bad things:
  - being hit by her mother
  - when her mother died

- having to look after her younger siblings

- when her father became depressed.

- Analyse the positive and negative aspects of Tina's childhood.

- Are there any issues you would have explored further with Tina?

- Are there any additional questions you would have asked?

- What do you consider to be the likely impact of Tina's childhood on her current behaviour in adult life?

EXERCISE 4 – CASE STUDY ON EDUCATION

❑ Paul attended Watts Junior and Infant School and Watts Town Comprehensive. He described them as ordinary schools. His attendance at Junior and Infant School and the first part of his comprehensive education was good.

❑ However, he reported missing quite a bit of school in his final few years and hardly attended at all during his last year at school. He made the following comments:

'I loved school when I was small, I was doing really well, I was near the top of the class.'

'As I got older, things started to get in the way...the arguments between my mam and her boyfriends.'

'When she started drinking things were really difficult... Sometimes I was so worried about her, I dare not leave her alone.'

❑ Paul considered himself to be an average pupil who was reasonably well-behaved.

❑ He was never in any serious trouble with his teachers, who he feels would have described him in the following terms:

'He could have done very well, but wasted his final years.'

'Sometimes he was really sad but never seemed able to talk to anyone about it.'

'Sometimes he was in a world of his own.'

'In his final year he just seemed to disappear.'

❑ Paul had a small circle of close friends. He remembers being very sad when his best friend's family moved away. For a while he felt extremely lonely.

❑ There was an occasion when another pupil tried to bully him but he stood up for himself. There was a group of pupils who caused quite a bit of trouble at school but Paul avoided them and never felt individually targeted.

❑ He feels that his friends would have described him in the following terms:

> 'He was a good friend...he was loyal.'

> 'He always had lots of pocket money...he was generous with us.'

❑ The worst thing that Paul did at school, apart from his non-attendance, was when he and two of his friends let the headmaster's car tyres down after one of their friends had been excluded from school for fighting.

❑ Paul was particularly good at sport and represented many of the school teams at football and athletics. He was really proud of this, it gave him a good feeling.

❑ Paul recognises that he could have done considerably better at school, particularly if he had applied himself in his final years. He did not take any examinations and deeply regrets this.

- Analyse the positive and negative features of Paul's education.

- Identify those aspects of Paul's education which are likely to have an impact upon him now.

- Are there any specific issues within Paul's education which may have a child protection implication?

- Is there anything which would require further clarification?

- Are there any other questions you would have asked?

EXERCISE 5 – CASE STUDY ON EMPLOYMENT

- ❑ Paul had a number of youth training schemes immediately after he left school, but all of these ended.

- ❑ He walked out of one of the schemes because he felt the employer was using them as 'slave labour'.

- ❑ He was unemployed for a little while and five years ago he obtained a job at a golf club approximately five miles away. Paul cycles there every day because of the expense of travelling.

- ❑ He really enjoys his job, although in the summer he has to work long hours and becomes very tired.

- ❑ In particular, Paul enjoys the National Vocational Training Courses which he goes on as part of his job.

- ❑ He has no ambition to be promoted, commenting, 'I don't think I could cope with the extra responsibility.'

- Assess the positive and negative aspects of Paul's employment.

- How might his work have an impact upon any child care responsibilities?

- Are there any issues raised by his employment which would require further investigation/clarification in other parts of the assessment?

- Are there any further questions you would have asked?

EXERCISE 6 – CASE STUDY ON PERCEPTION OF SELF

In the book's main case study, Michelle's perception of herself does not give cause for much optimism.

There are, however, cases where parents respond very differently to the intervention of child protection agencies and their actions lead them to have a very different perception of themselves.

The following exercise presumes that Michelle responded to child protection concerns by separating from John. She then described herself very differently.

- ❑ Michelle described herself in the following terms:

    'I like to be quiet.'

    'I am not one for crowds.'

'I am not very good at some things...but I believe I am getting better.'

'I used to be very nervous on my own, but since I began to work with the Family Centre, I am getting better.'

'I would do anything for anyone...but I am beginning to realise that people have taken advantage of me.'

'I used not to have very much confidence, but I am becoming much more assertive now.'

'I have more pride in myself since I left John.'

'I feel really determined now... Before, I would just have accepted things.'

❑ Michelle considers that her best feature is 'the changes I have made...the things I have achieved in the past six months', and the things she likes least about herself, 'that I am too fat', and 'that I made such a mess of things...especially being with John...and allowing all of those things to happen to David.'

❑ She is happy when:

'I think about all the progress I have made since I separated from John.'

'I see David.'

'I have some time to myself...a time to just sit and think.'

The last time she was happy was the last contact she had with David and next time she will be happy is when she sees him again tomorrow.

The happiest she has ever been in her life was when she gave birth to David.

Michelle says she feels much happier now than she has in recent years, she feels much more positive about herself and much more confident than when she was with John. She believes that she is much happier now because her life is no longer in a mess and she feels she has a much more promising future to look forward to.

When she is happy she tends to smile a lot and is generally much more sociable.

❑ The following things make her angry:

'realising the mess I have made of things'

'allowing David to be injured'

'getting involved with John'

'Sometimes the social workers... They don't seem to realise how much progress I have made in the last six months.'

'I get angry with myself sometimes... I feel that I could be doing things better than I do.'

'When I talk about my childhood with the psychologist... I feel angry about some of the things that happened to me.'

Michelle recognises that sometimes in the past she has let her angry feelings out immediately and this has not always been helpful to her or David. She can now see that her angry behaviour upset and distressed David. She also realises that she became angry with people who were trying to help her, for example, the health visitor. She now feels that she is able to manage her angry feelings much more appropriately. She has already started her 'anger management course' and this is enabling her to avoid angry situations, manage her anger in a different fashion and redirect her anger more positively. She commented that when she had been angry the previous week she had used the angry energy by redecorating David's bedroom.

There are still occasions when she has to walk away from situations because she can feel her anger developing.

Michelle believes that her anger has reduced significantly in the last six months. She attributes this to her separation from John, the anger management course, the work with the psychologist about her childhood, and her much more positive outlook on life.

❑ The following things make Michelle sad:

'When I have to say goodbye to David.'

'Sometimes because of what happened to me when I was a child.'

'I feel sad when David is sad.'

The saddest time in her life was when David was removed from her care.

When she is sad, she usually cries.

She believes that she is generally less sad now than previously.

❑ Michelle believes that people would describe her in the following terms:

'She has made a mess of things...but she is beginning to get things back together.'

'She can be stubborn when she has made her mind up about things.'

'She will do anything for anybody...sometimes people take advantage of her.'

'She smiles more now than she used to.'

'She has made a lot of mistakes in the past.'

'Not everything was her fault.'

❑ Michelle now believes that her life revolves around David and this is her motivation to sort herself out. She feels proud of herself and the changes she has made. She recognises that she still has a long way to go and realises she is going to make mistakes from time to time.

❑ In twelve months' time she would like to be looking after David, and to have kept John out of her life.

❑ In three years time she would like to be looking after David with no social services department involvement in her life.

• Evaluate Michelle's perception of herself.

• In what ways do you feel that her perception of herself reduces the level of child protection concerns?

• What issues would you have explored further with her?

• What additional questions would you have asked?

EXERCISE 7 – CASE STUDY ON SELF-ESTEEM

Donna has had her four children removed from her care because she has an alcohol abuse problem which has resulted in the children being neglected, frequently left to look after themselves, and living in dirty and unhygienic conditions.

Donna's answers to questions indicated that her self-esteem was poor.

❑ Generally she is not very sure of herself.

❑ She would find it very difficult to make a speech.

- ❑ There are lots of things she would change about herself, for example, her abuse of alcohol.

- ❑ She does not have a great deal of confidence in her decisions.

- ❑ She feels ashamed of things she has done in the past, for example neglecting the children and drinking too much.

- ❑ She does not feel that photographs do her justice.

- ❑ She thinks family members make her feel she is not good enough, particularly her parents. She gets upset if someone criticises her.

- ❑ She is likely to remain silent because she feels people laugh at what she says.

- ❑ She is shy in social situations.

- ❑ She is not happy with the way she looks.

- ❑ She does not feel she is physically attractive.

Donna answered 'Don't know' or 'Sometimes' in the following areas of self-esteem:

- ❑ Does not know if she often thinks she is a failure, but sometimes she thinks she is.

- ❑ Sometimes she wishes she were someone else.

- ❑ Sometimes she is shy with other people because she thinks she will be rejected.

- ❑ Sometimes she finds it difficult to do things in a way which other people think is good.

- How would you evaluate Donna's self-esteem?

- In what areas – for example, her social interactions, interpersonal relationships or perception of self – would you say her self-esteem is adversely affected?

EXERCISE 8 – CASE STUDY ON RIGID/FLEXIBLE, ORGANISED/DISORGANISED THINKING AND BEHAVIOUR

Pauline and Jason live with their four children, Jason (junior) aged 5, Paul aged 3, Darren aged 2 and Chantelle aged 6 months, in a two-bedroom flat.

Concern has been expressed because Jason (junior) often arrives at school late and has seldom had any breakfast. Paul has not been attending the 'Tiny Tots Nursery' place which was provided when he was assessed as being a child in need, and Chantelle has been missing hospital appointments.

The home is usually untidy, and in particular the kitchen often contains the remains of previous meals littered on work surfaces. All of the children have recently been treated for head lice and scabies. The children are frequently bruised as a result of falling over the clutter in the flat.

Pauline's responses to the checklist were:

- ☐ I would like to be organised but things do not work out that way. I always seem to be rushing around and never getting anything done. As soon as I have tidied one thing up the kids have messed something else up.

- ☐ Jason doesn't help, he mends bits of his car in the flat, and leaves them lying around.

- ☐ If I don't know what is going to happen next, I tend to get into a bit of a panic. I end up shouting at the kids.

- ☐ If something suddenly crops up I had not expected, I can get angry. Jason is the opposite, he just says not to worry, we'll manage.

  I can't always manage, last week the hospital appointment came for Chantelle the day before she had to go. I could not get things sorted out to take her.

  Jason doesn't help, he's useless.

- ☐ If things aren't planned I panic, but I never have the time to plan anything. I feel angry.

- ☐ I would love to follow the same routines but that's impossible here. Something always crops up to upset things.

- ☐ I never know what is going to happen next, I get really stressed.

- ☐ We need a daily routine but we don't have one.

  In the morning it takes all of my energy to stop the kids fighting with each other...getting them dressed is a nightmare.

Jason is always in bed until lunch time.

- ❑ There's not a lot I can do if the routine is disrupted, I just try my best.

- ❑ I lose my temper with the kids because things are never organised, but I know that doesn't help. I just get so tired sometimes.

- ❑ I try to give myself plenty of time to get to places but by the time I have the kids organised we always seem to be late for things. Things always go wrong.

- ❑ Things always get disrupted in this house so there is no point in getting wound up about it…but I do.

- ❑ There is no point in doing anything if something we have planned goes wrong… It would just go wrong again if we tried to do it.

- ❑ I like not to change my mind about things but that is not always easy. Sometimes I have to give in to keep the peace with Jason.

Sometimes the kids go on and on and I am too tired to say no.

- ❑ I would love the children to have the same routines but they are too much for me. They know they have me running round after them.

- ❑ I try to make them do things, like going to bed so they won't be tired in the morning, but they just play me up.

Jason (junior) is always too tired for school because he sits and watches the TV in his bedroom all night.

- ❑ Jason does not help.

He says that he used to do his own thing when he was little and it hasn't done him any harm.

He thinks children should be free spirits.

He thinks we should live day to day.

He does not like things to be organised, he says he gets bored if things are the same every day…that's what he hated most about prison.

- ❑ When we only had Jason (junior) and Paul it was better, I seemed to be able to manage then.

Jason used to help a bit more.

My mother used to come round most days and I could manage then. She stopped coming so much after she met George...he's her new boyfriend.

- ❏ I don't know what we would need to change or how we could change things.

- Comment on the ways in which Pauline is organised, and how this impacts on the care of the children.

- Comment on the ways in which she is disorganised, and how this impacts on the care of the children.

- Are there any answers you would have explored further?

- Are there any additional questions you would have asked?

- What risks to the children are implied by these answers?

EXERCISE 9 – CASE STUDY ON DOMINANT AND SUBMISSIVE BEHAVIOUR

Alison is 23 years of age. She has a daughter, Aimee, who is 2 months old. Aimee recently suffered a fractured skull. Other injuries included bruising to her ribs and haemorrhaging of the blood vessels in her eyes. The consultant paediatrician who examined Aimee diagnosed non-accidental injury consistent with a gripping, shaking, impact event. At the time the injuries were sustained, Aimee's father Clive was looking after her.

Clive initially agreed to leave the family home but now wants to return. He denies injuring Aimee and insists she banged her head when he slipped on the stairs.

Alison is being assessed to see if she can parent Aimee by herself, and in particular whether she is able to protect her daughter.

Alison's responses to the checklist were:

- ❏ I am a reasonably confident person.

- ❏ I like to do things my way if given the choice ... sometimes that is not possible.

- ❏ I would stand up for myself if I thought I was right, but I would still listen to what the other person was saying.

- ❏ It would depend who I was arguing with and what the issue was. I would not argue with someone just to make a point, but if I was being accused of something I had not done or being blamed for something unfairly, I would not back down. If it was something about Aimee I would probably argue.

□ I would not argue with someone if I thought I was wrong.

□ I think I mostly only argue if I think it is important, although I sometimes argue if I am in a bad mood.

I would argue if I thought people were trying to take advantage of me.

□ If I think I am wrong I would probably admit it, but maybe not immediately.

□ I might apologise, but maybe not immediately.

I don't usually end up being in charge of things, I prefer to remain in the crowd.

I don't particularly like being told what to do by people who are full of their own importance.

If people try to take over I will stop them if I think it is important.

People who want to be in charge of things don't bother me.

I won't let people be in charge of me.

I will fight against people who want to take over my life... I don't try to control them, so why should they want to control me?

□ I can be nervous in new situations or with strangers, but I don't think I am any more nervous than most people.

□ Some decisions are difficult and some are easy.

I don't have a real difficulty in making decisions... I worry sometimes in case I have not made the right decision and sometimes I get it wrong.

I found it difficult to decide that Clive can't live with us any more... I still love him.

I found the decision about Aimee and Clive easy, she must always come first.

□ Clive used to make some important decisions for me, but not any more.

□ Showing emotions is not a sign of weakness.

□ I would like people to apologise to me if they are in the wrong but I would not insist.

If they don't I will not have much respect for them in the future.

☐ I don't become angry with people to make my point.

I will raise my voice to make my point if I feel that I am not being listened to.

☐ Crying is not a sign of weakness, but I know some people who think it is.

- Describe Alison's dominant aspects.
- Describe Alison's submissive aspects.
- Have you any concerns about Alison's ability to protect Aimee?
- Would you have asked any further questions?
- Would you have further explored any of the answers?

EXERCISE 10 – CASE STUDY ON ALCOHOL ABUSE

Geoff is 26 years of age. He is in a relationship with Sarah which is characterised by violence. Sarah's daughter, Amber, aged 6, has witnessed the violence and recently she was bruised on the face when she intervened in a violent incident.

Geoff's responses to the checklist were:

☐ I started to drink when I was 14 or 15. There were a gang of us, we would drink in the local park.

I would get drunk, all of us did.

Drinking...it made me feel one of the lads.

☐ I have drunk on and off all my life...sometimes I get drunk.

I'm not an alcoholic.

I went through a period before I met Sarah when I hardly drunk at all.

☐ I have phases when I don't have any...and then times when I drink a lot.

At the moment I'm drinking a lot...but I can handle it.

I have about two bottles of cider...the strong stuff...and as many cans of lager as I can afford... It is the only way I can cope with all the hassle.

I'm drinking most days at the moment... It's Sarah, she does my head in...

- ❑ I drink at home… I sometimes go off by myself with a bottle. I don't have anyone in particular who I drink with.

- ❑ I used to pass out from drink when I was younger. I run out of money before I pass out now.

- ❑ My mood can be different… It depends.

  Sometimes I get angry…especially with Sarah… She goes on at me when I have had a drink… She doesn't understand.

  I'm probably more violent when I have had a drink…especially if people are winding me up.

- ❑ I spend my jobseekers allowance, usually within a couple of days… Then Sarah gives me some…sometimes.

  My mates help me out.

  When I'm drinking I spend every penny on booze.

- ❑ I've sold things in the past to buy booze. Sarah won't let me now. We argue about it…sometimes things get out of hand.

- ❑ I drink to forget…things don't seem so bad when I'm drunk. It helps me to relax.

  I get stressed out sometimes…the booze helps.

  I like the feeling…it makes me more confident.

  I'm not an alcoholic. I don't drink in the morning like they do.

  I can give up any time I want.

  Sometimes I think I should drink less…it's difficult though.

- ❑ I tend to drink alone.

- ❑ I look after myself okay when I am drinking. I have to…Sarah doesn't help me when I've had a bit too much.

- ❑ I've had no physical problems.

  I went to a psychiatrist once. The court sent me when I was having a bad time…drinking. They said I needed help… She just talked, it did no good.

- ❑ I've had a bit to drink when I've had Amber…but I can always manage her… I know what I'm doing even when I'm drunk.

❏ She looks after me sometimes when I've had too much... She makes me cups of tea and things.

- How would you describe Geoff's alcohol use?

- Comment on the impact of his alcohol use on his relationship with Sarah and Amber.

- Does Geoff's use of alcohol give rise to child protection concerns?

- Are there any answers you would have explored further?

- Are there any additional questions you would have asked?

EXERCISE 11 – CASE STUDY ON DRUG ABUSE

Joanne is 26 years of age. Her first two children were removed following allegations of neglect. It was found that they had experienced a chaotic lifestyle. The relationship between Joanne and her ex-partner Clive was characterised by violence and the parents were both using heroin on a regular basis.

Despite a promise to give up heroin, Joanne and Clive continued to misuse drugs.

Her two children were subsequently freed for adoption.

Joanne then became pregnant again, and because of previous concerns the new baby has been made subject to care proceedings.

Joanne reported the following drug history.

❏ **Amphetamine sulphate**

Joanne used amphetamine sulphate between the ages of 16 and 19. She was an occasional user, she never injected and it was administered orally in a cup of coffee. She reported the following effects:

'It made me really alert.'

'You feel that everything is going faster than it really is.'

'Being up was okay.'

'Coming down was a real drop.'

'I wasn't really into it that much.'

She stopped using amphetamine sulphate because the effect of the drug wearing off made her feel low in mood and she became extremely tearful.

□ **Heroin**

Joanne reported that she started using heroin approximately two years ago. Initially she was smoking it, but when she could no longer get the buzz she was after she started injecting.

Joanne gave up when she discovered she was pregnant with Paul, and reports that she has not used it since then.

She began to attend a community-based drug counselling and support service, and went immediately onto a methadone programme. She started on 55 mls a day, was maintained at 35 mls during her pregnancy, and since the birth of Paul has reduced to 30 mls.

Joanne has provided weekly urine samples as a part of her methadone programme and these have been negative from when she started ten months ago.

Joanne reported that heroin had the following effect for her:

'It made me feel drowsy.'

'It gave me a warm feeling.'

'After I started injecting I got high quicker and it lasted longer.'

'Injecting gave me a real buzz.'

'Coming down was really bad.'

Joanne made the following comments about her drug misuse:

'We weren't living, we were just surviving.'

'When I got pregnant I said we had to give up for the sake of the baby... Clive wouldn't... I had to chose between him and the baby. I chose the baby.'

'It was really difficult in the beginning... I was tempted loads of times... Sometimes the pain and the cramps were almost unbearable.'

'I am okay with the methadone programme.. I am coming off that slowly.'

'I lost Daniel and Clare. I am not prepared to lose Paul.'

'I don't want to do it any more.'

'It's not worth the hassle. You just wake up in the morning. You want a bag... It is so degrading.'

'In the beginning it made me feel good. At the end I needed it just to feel normal.'

'I am really proud of myself for what I have done. I am worth something now.'

'I used to hate myself for the way I was. I am slowly getting my self-respect back.'

(The information which she has given has been confirmed by the community based drug project which supports her).

- Evaluate the information which Joanne has provided.

- What do you believe to be the current risks?

- What is your view about whether or not Paul should be returned to live with his mother?

- Are there any further questions you would have asked?

- Are there any answers you would have explored further?

- If Paul is returned to live with his mother, what support and monitoring arrangements would be necessary in order to safeguard and promote Paul's welfare?

EXERCISE 12 – CASE STUDY ON AGGRESSIVE TENDENCIES

Paul and Mandy have two children, Sean aged 7 and Patrick aged 5. Sean has recently disclosed that Mandy's step-father has sexually abused him. Paul has found this extremely difficult to come to terms with, especially as it has reminded him of the sexual abuse he suffered when he was a child.

He made the following responses to the checklist.

- ❑ It would depend on what they did to me...whether or not I would get my revenge on them.

  If it was something little I probably wouldn't bother.

  If it was something big I would get them. It would be worse than they got me.

  If it was something against the kids I would do them good.

- ❑ No, I would not let them know I was after them and I would make sure they could not prove it was me after I had done them.

❑ If I was really angry I could do somebody some harm.

❑ I tend to lash out with anything that comes to hand.

❑ I used to hurt myself a lot when I was younger.

   I have burned myself with cigarettes. I have cut myself. I blamed myself for what my dad did to me. I thought it was my fault.

   I don't think of hurting myself now.

❑ If someone insulted me I would probably ignore them, unless they went on and on, and then I would probably start back on them.

❑ Yes, I really want to hurt Mandy's stepdad.

   I'll get him… He knows that. He knows what I am like.

❑ I watch violent films…but it's all pretend, isn't it?

❑ I am okay about seeing blood, so long as it's not mine.

❑ I yell and swear all the time when I get angry.

❑ I get angry all the time since this happened to Sean.

❑ I swore at Mandy yesterday because the kids were making too much noise.

❑ If people let me down I don't forgive them.

❑ I got involved in some fights when I was growing up… Everybody does.

   I was bullied a lot when I was young… You learn to run or fight… I learned to fight.

❑ No, not unless they are really in my face. I might give them a smack then.

❑ Not all people who refuse to fight are cowards.

   Sometimes you have to fight so that people know they can't push you around.

❑ I am angry more often than most people now…since what happened to Sean.

❑ I have a lot of anger in me. Sometimes I even scare myself.

❑ I don't smash things when I am angry… I never have.

- ☐ The most violent thing I have ever done was to hit this bloke with a bat. He was after me because he thought I grassed him up, it was me or him, I made sure it was him.

- ☐ Yes, I would do the same again if it was going to save me from being beaten up.

- ☐ If someone was prodding me in the chest, I would hit them.

- ☐ I get angry when people upset me, but this does not mean I get violent.

- ☐ I sometimes get angry with people who get on my nerves, doesn't everybody.

- ☐ If it was a friend who was making fun of me I would make fun of them.

  If it was someone I did not know I would want to know what they were at... If they wanted trouble they could have it.

  If it was someone I did not like I would have a go at them.

- ☐ People who are showing off are okay so long as they don't do it at my expense.

- ☐ I have two convictions for violence...but it wasn't my fault.

  I have been arrested another twice but never charged. They were both arguments with Mandy that got out of hand, she refused to press charges after she had calmed down and had time to think about it.

- ☐ I'm not aggressive...unless I have to be.

  If people start on me I will let them have it.

- ☐ People don't show respect if they think you can't look after yourself.

- ☐ I have been violent but I am not a violent person.

- ☐ Other people probably see me as someone who can look after himself but does not go looking for trouble.

  People know I can look after myself in a fight...so some people avoid me and others want to have a go... It's their choice, not mine.

- Evaluate the extent of Paul's aggressive tendencies.

- How do you feel the aggressive tendencies would impact upon the care of the children?

- How do you feel the aggressive tendencies impact upon family relationships?

- Are there any further issues in respect of Paul's aggressive tendencies which need to be explored?

- Do any of the answers need further clarification?

EXERCISE 13 – CASE STUDY FOR ACCEPTING RESPONSIBILITY FOR ANGRY/VIOLENT BEHAVIOUR

- ❏ No, I don't blame drinking or taking drugs for my violence.

- ❏ Drinking doesn't help… I know that I will lose it more quickly if I have had a drink.

- ❏ Threatening people is sometimes the only way to get things done.

- ❏ Yes…once I start the red haze comes down. I get pretty wild.

- ❏ I sometimes don't remember what I have done when I have lost it.

- ❏ My father was violent sometimes, but not the same as me.

- ❏ My parents never really got violent with each other.

- ❏ A lot of the parents around where we lived used to smack each other all the time.

- ❏ I only get angry because people wind me up.

- ❏ I never start on them first…but I never walk away from trouble.

- ❏ I suppose it is the way I am made. I have always been like this.

- ❏ I only get violent when people wind me up.

- ❏ Sometimes people exaggerate the damage I have done, but not always.

- ❏ I never used to think it was my fault when I became violent. Now I wonder sometimes.

- ❏ I thought about changing sometimes…but it is difficult. People expect me to be like this…what can I do?

- Evaluate these answers.

- Are there any additional questions you would have asked?

- Are there any answers you would have clarified?

EXERCISE 14 – CASE STUDY FOR ANGER/VIOLENCE WITHIN THE ADULT RELATIONSHIP – PERPETRATOR

☐ When I lose my temper I sometimes say things to make Mandy feel small.

Sometimes she winds me up so I have a go at her.

☐ I don't demand to be answered... Mandy always answers me when I talk to her.

☐ We all say things to hurt and upset each other when we have lost our temper. Isn't that what arguments are all about? It's part of winning an argument, isn't it?

☐ I have chased Mandy a few times ... but only when she really winds me up.

Yes, I have grabbed her in anger.

Yes, I have given her a whack a couple of times... but nothing really hard.

☐ I have never kicked Mandy. Only cowards kick people.

I don't throw things. I never have.

I have never used a weapon against Mandy.

☐ I have had Mandy round the neck a couple of times, but nothing serious. It was just to make the point to her.

There is very little violence in our house. We get on okay.

The last time was ages ago, I can't remember the details.

People keep going on about all this violence between me and Mandy... They exaggerate.

There was some violence in the past, but not now.

We have both calmed down a lot. They are becoming less frequent.

☐ I hit Mandy when I lose it.

Sometimes I just get so wound up. I have a lot of anger inside me.

I know I don't have the right to hit Mandy, but sometimes I just lose it.

Sometimes it is as if she is just asking for it.

❑ Mandy is okay...she gets upset if I have given her a smack. When she has calmed down she is okay. She knows that I don't mean it.

❑ Yes, I would probably continue being violent sometimes. It's how I'm made.

❑ Sometimes I would like to be different with Mandy. Sometimes I feel really bad afterwards.

They have talked about me going on one of these anger management courses. I am not sure it would do any good.

Maybe I will try one. I don't know.

- Evaluate Paul's violent tendencies.

- Are there any of Paul's responses which you would have explored further?

- Are there any additional questions you would have asked?

- Do you feel that there is anything which might enable Paul to be less violent within the relationship?

EXERCISE 15 – CASE STUDY ON SCHEDULE 1 OFFENCES

Cheryl is 20 years of age. She has a daughter, Lisa, aged 4. When Lisa was 2 Cheryl was convicted of assault on her daughter. Cheryl had smacked Lisa when she found her striking matches in her bedroom. Lisa had severe bruising on her buttocks and legs.

Cheryl's answers to the checklist questions were as follows.

❑ I was eighteen years old at the time of the offence and Lisa was two.

I've grown up a lot since then.

❑ Lisa is my daughter and I have always looked after her.

Her father has never been around to help me.

❑ Lisa had seen me using matches to light the gas fire and a couple of times I had found her trying to get the box off the mantelpiece. I had told her... I had explained to her how dangerous matches were. She could be defiant little madam then. I sometimes think she invented the terrible twos.

This one particular day I had put her upstairs for a nap. I could hear her giggling and went to find out what was happening. She was striking matches and dropping them onto the bed. I lost it completely. I imagined her whole bedroom going up in flames.

I couldn't believe what I had done to her...when I looked...all those bruises on her little bottom.

I took her to my mother's straightaway. I phoned the social services department and told them what I had done.

❑ Lisa went to live with my mother for a little while.

I was given two years' probation. The probation officer was really helpful...and the social worker... I started going to a family centre. I did an anger management course. That helped a lot.

❑ Yes, I know I am a Schedule 1 offender. I am ashamed about that...but I have to live with it.

I still get angry and upset with Lisa sometimes...but never like that... I would manage it very differently now.

I don't think I pose a risk to Lisa...but I know that they still keep an eye on me. I suppose I have to live with that.

- Analyse Cheryl's Schedule 1 offence.
- Do you believe that Cheryl poses a risk to her daughter Lisa?
- Are there any further questions you would have asked?
- Would you have further clarified any of the answers?

EXERCISE 16 – CASE STUDY FOR SCHEDULE 1 OFFENCES

Gordon is 45. He recently established a relationship with Tanya, who is 18 and suffers from moderate learning disability. Tanya is now pregnant, and a child protection case conference recommended an assessment of Gordon because of his Schedule 1 offence.

He gave the following answers to the checklist questions.

❑ It was so long ago... I can't really remember the details.

I was about twenty-five...I think.

They said she was twelve but she looked about eighteen. She acted really grown up.

❑ Yes I knew her...she lived in the village.

I knew her mother. She was older than me. I fancied her.

I had seen them out playing a few times.

I would say hello if we met in the street. We got chatting.

Eventually I would see her almost every day. She knew I fancied her. I would walk round that way to the pub... She and her mates would come running over. They were always borrowing fags from me.

I can't really remember what happened.

We had sex...that was it.

She was the one who did all the running.

It didn't last long...just a couple of times.

Nobody else was involved. It wasn't like that... We would just go off into the woods.

We stopped because she thought she was pregnant and told her mother.

❑ The police came round and arrested me. They said it was under-age sex and I was in trouble... They said I was a pervert.

In court they said I had sexually abused her.

They said she had learning disability... But that's not true. She was a bit slow, that was all.

She knew what was happening... It wasn't abuse... She consented... She enjoyed it as much as me.

I got two years in prison. I should not have got sent down.

It was just a bit of fun. She didn't get harmed. I was locked up with blokes who had interfered with little children.

❑ They had some course inside which I went to. They said it would reduce my sentence.

I didn't really learn anything. It wasn't meant for me... It was for people who messed about with children.

I know about Schedule 1 offenders, they say I am one...but I aren't really.

Being a Schedule 1 offender isn't right. I shouldn't be one.

I met a couple of blokes in prison who I still see sometimes. One of them used to beat up his son. The other one interfered with little girls. We get together every now and again and drink.

❑ Sometimes you see young lasses that you fancy…but everybody does.

I wouldn't do anything now…not since I met Tanya… She gives me everything I need.

❑ I was arrested a couple of years ago, they said I had been messing around with this eight-year-old girl where I used to babysit.

I used to bounce her up and down on my knee but that was all.

She said that I had touched her…but I didn't… If I did it was only accidental.

❑ No I am not a risk to children… All this about me and Tanya is nonsense. I don't pose any risk to the baby at all.

- Evaluate the risk which Gordon would present to his children.

- Are there any additional questions you would have asked?

- Are there any answers which Gordon gave which you would have explored further?

EXERCISE 17 – CASE STUDY FOR CRIMINAL HISTORY

Paul and Tina have two children. John is 5 and Samantha is 3.

Their combined parenting skills have previously provided a good enough, safe enough level of care for the children. However, Tina struggles to manage the children by herself. She feels unsupported by Paul and sometimes loses her temper with the children. There has recently been a Section 47 investigation where Samantha was found to have bruising to her buttocks and thighs. Tina admitted to smacking Samantha because she had been swearing. At the time Paul was on remand in prison.

Tina has no criminal convictions. Paul, who is 25 years of age, reported the following criminal history.

❑ At 17 years of age he was put on probation for receiving a stolen pedal cycle.

❑ At 18 he was fined and put on probation when he admitted four offences of taking a motor vehicle without consent.

- ❑ At 19 years of age he served six months' Youth Custody for six offences of taking motor vehicles without consent.

- ❑ At 21 years of age he served a prison sentence of four months following conviction for receiving and handling stolen property.

- ❑ At 22 years of age he was sentenced to six months in prison for theft of motor vehicle and handling stolen goods. He was banned from driving for three years.

- ❑ At 23 years of age he was sent to prison for three months for driving whilst disqualified.

- ❑ At 23 years of age he was sentenced to three months in prison for driving whilst disqualified.

- ❑ At 24 years of age he was sent to prison for three months for driving whilst disqualified.

- ❑ At 24 years of age he was sent to prison for six months for driving whilst disqualified and receiving stolen goods.

- ❑ He is currently banned from driving until he is 35 years of age.

- Evaluate the impact of Paul's criminal history on his family life, and its impact on the care of the children.

- What child protection concerns are raised as a result of Paul's criminal history?

- If, when Paul was 19, he had received a conviction for assault occasioning actual bodily harm, which resulted from a dispute with a neighbour, what concerns would you have?

- What would your concerns be if Paul had a conviction for assaulting Tina the previous year?

- What would your concerns be if Tina or Paul had two convictions for possession of drugs?

- Would your concerns be heightened if they had convictions for dealing in drugs, and if so, why?

- What would your concerns be if Paul had a conviction for assault on a fifteen-year-old girl?

EXERCISE 18 – CASE STUDY FOR PREVIOUS RELATIONSHIPS

Andy is 34 years of age and lives alone.

He has one child from a previous relationship with Sarah. As the result of a one-night stand he now has a baby son, Ben, who is two months old. Ben has been removed from his mother's care because she has formed a relationship with a Schedule 1 offender. Andy wants Ben to live with him.

Andy's answers to the checklist questions were:

- ☐ I have been a bit of a lad in the past... I have never really had any serious relationships.

  I have never lived with any of the women I have been going out with.

  I prefer to have a relationship where we both have our own houses... that way we can have some personal space. Otherwise people get on each other's nerves.

  I suppose the only really serious relationship was with Sarah.

  I think we were both about 22 when we met.

  I was working on a building site at the time. I was earning loads of money... I had a nice flat. I had no worries.

  We met in a night club in town.

  I thought she looked really gorgeous... She was dressed to kill.

  She laughed all the time...she liked a good joke.

  She was good fun to be with.

- ☐ The relationship lasted on and off for about two years.

  We would have times when we were always together and then other times when we did our own thing for a while.

  We didn't really live together although we spent a lot of time staying at each other's flats.

- ☐ Andy described Sarah in the following terms:

  'She was good fun.'

  'She could be a little bit over the top sometimes.'

  'When she was in a good mood...she was a real laugh.'

  'When she was in a bad mood she could be argumentative.'

  'She was all right for a while...then she would get on my nerves.'

'She used to drink too much.'

The best thing about Sarah was, 'She was a good laugh', and her worst aspect was 'After a while she got on my nerves.'

□ We have a son, Joshua. He will be six now.

Our relationship finished before Joshua was born.

After he was born I would go and see him but Sarah could be awkward about the arrangements. She would not let me take Joshua out.

Eventually she said I couldn't see Joshua any more. She had a new bloke. I got in the way.

I don't see Joshua now. I thought about going to court about it ... but there was no point.

□ I think our relationship ended because I still wanted my freedom, but Sarah wanted to settle down. She is settled down with her new partner. She seems happy.

□ Looking back, I think that I did the right thing. I was not ready to settle down then.

□ I miss not seeing Joshua, but that is the price you have to pay.

• Evaluate Andy's previous relationship.

• Are there any questions you would have asked?

• Would you have clarified further any of his answers?

EXERCISE 19 – CASE STUDY FOR PRESENT RELATIONSHIP

Pauline and Josh live in a two-bedroom terraced house with Pauline's children: Joseph, aged 4, and Ben, aged 2.

Pauline left her previous relationship because of domestic violence and the children were on the child protection register because Joseph had been injured during a violent domestic dispute.

Pauline's responses to the checklist were:

□ I met Josh about eighteen months ago.

We met at the local laundrette. I was having difficulty managing Joseph and Ben and the washing. Josh gave me a hand.

We have lived together for about nine months... It was a slow courtship... I was really nervous about men after my previous experience.

I was first attracted by his kindness. He is probably the first person I have met who thinks of others before he thinks of himself.

□ Pauline described Josh in the following terms:

'He might not be beautiful on the outside, but he is beautiful on the inside.'

'He always puts others before himself.'

'He can be a bit grumpy first thing in the morning.'

'He is terrific with Joseph and Ben.'

'He is so patient.'

'He can be really untidy sometimes.'

She described his best feature as 'He always thinks of others before he thinks of himself', and his worst aspect as 'He always thinks of others before he thinks of himself. Sometimes people take advantage of him and he does not see it.'

My parents approve of him, they wish I had met him before I met the boys' father.

□ We tend to share the jobs around the house, although if I am not careful Josh monopolises the boys and I end up doing all of the domestic chores.

I think that we make important decisions together.

I have to be careful because Josh will always let me have my own way.

We normally agree about most things and if something is really important we will sit down and talk about it.

We sometimes disagree because I think Josh spoils Joseph and Ben. He should not give in to them all the time.

If we disagree, Josh usually gives in and lets me have my own way.

□ I organise the bills and the money.

That is not something I insist upon...it is just something that has happened.

❏ I feel that Josh has a great respect for me.

Of course I have respect for him...it's mutual.

I believe that he always listens to me.

Josh has never hurt me in any way...that is so important after my previous relationship.

Sometimes he can be a little bit insensitive with the things he says...but he is never malicious...he never intends to hurt me.

If I could change something about Josh I would make him more assertive.

❏ I can't see there is anything which would prevent us staying together for the rest of our lives.

If we did ever separate...I don't know what I would do... I can't imagine being in a better relationship than this one.

I am very happy with my relationship.

It would be even more perfect if we had a child of our own.

Josh will know what I have said about our relationship... We talk about it all the time. He knows how I think and how I feel.

- Evaluate the relationship between Josh and Pauline.

- Are there any further questions you would have asked?

- Is there any clarification you would have sought from the answers given?

- Would you consider that there are any child protection concerns raised by these answers?

EXERCISE 20 – CASE STUDY FOR STATEMENTS ABOUT THE RELATIONSHIP WITH YOUR CURRENT PARTNER

Josh listed the following as the priorities in respect of his relationship with Pauline:

1. I love her.

2. She loves me.

3. I trust her.

4. She makes me feel wanted.

5.   She looks after me.

6.   She is a good friend.

7.   She is a good parent.

8.   Without her I would feel lonely.

9.   She is a good cook.

10. She is good with money.

11. She lets me have personal space when I need it.

12. She lets me go out with friends.

13. She lets me spend money on myself.

14. I don't want to start over again with someone else.

15. I need a woman in my life.

- Evaluate this information.

EXERCISE 21 – CASE STUDY ON PERCEPTION OF CHILDREN

Pauline's answers to the checklist questions in respect of Joseph were as follows:

- ☐ Pauline described Joseph in the following terms:

    'He is a lovely little lad.'

    'He is very bubbly.'

    'He is very loving...towards Ben, me and Josh.'

    'Joseph and me clash sometimes...but he protects me.'

    'They are good kids.'

    'If you are doing something in the house, Joseph always wants to help you.'

    'He can be naughty sometimes.'

    'Sometimes he does not want to go to bed... Sometimes he has little tantrums.'

    She described his best feature as 'He is so loving', and she least likes him when 'He will not do as he is told'.

☐ Pauline feels that Joseph is happy most of the time, and in particular he is happy when he is playing.

He is unhappy sometimes when he can't get his own way but he is easily distracted and his unhappiness does not last for very long.

☐ Pauline does not believe that Joseph is an angry little boy.

He has his temper tantrums…but no more than other children, and probably less than most.

He was more angry when she was in her previous relationship.

She dealt with his temper tantrums by ignoring him.

Sometimes Josh gives in to him and they have words.

Pauline feels that Joseph was an angry little boy because of his experiences when Pauline was living with her previous partner, but she believes that he is now recovering from that.

☐ Pauline feels that Josh sometimes spoils Joseph and she tries to compensate for that.

She believes that Joseph knows he can wind Josh around his little finger. Sometimes he ignores her and goes straight to Josh, because he knows he will get his own way.

- Evaluate Pauline's perception of Joseph.

- Are there any answers which you would have explored further?

- Are there any additional questions you would have asked?

EXERCISE 22 – CASE STUDY FOR PERCEPTIONS OF PARENTING

Margaret lives with her partner, John, and their daughter Charlotte, aged 3 years. The nursery made a referral because Charlotte had a number of bruises. She told the nursery staff that her 'dad' had smacked her.

A paediatric assessment identified bruising of three different ages and possibly more.

John responded with the following answers to the checklist.

☐ Being a parent is easy most of the time.
Sometimes it is difficult, especially when she is playing up.

The easiest thing is when she is in a good mood and she does as she is told.

The most difficult thing is when she won't do as she is told.

☐ I like being a parent most of the time.

The best thing is playing with her...when she is okay.

I like it when people know I am a father.

The best thing is knowing I am her dad.

☐ The worst thing is when I am tired and I run out of patience.

When she goes on and on.

When I can't get any peace and quiet.

☐ Not really...I don't think I could do anything better as a parent.

Sometimes I wish I had more patience.

☐ I don't know...this is my first child.

She was okay when she was a baby. She was an easy baby.

☐ I don't know really. I will take it as it comes.

Probably teenagers because they can be a bit of a pain.

☐ Being there for them.

Playing with them.

Keeping a roof over their heads.

☐ I shout at Margaret to see to her when she cries.

☐ She doesn't come to me for much really...only if Margaret is not around. She sometimes comes and shows me things.

☐ I shout Margaret if Charlotte needs comforting.

☐ I don't think I have made mistakes as a parent.

☐ Nothing...I have not been hitting Charlotte... I give her the odd tap when she has been naughty or when she is being a pain.

Her mother lets her get away with everything... That's the problem.

Charlotte can wrap her mother round her little finger.

☐ No, nothing has happened to Charlotte which I regret.

I regret the social services department becoming involved.

I regret I don't have more money to pay the bills.

- □ School is important. I would make her go.

  I wasted my education, I don't want Charlotte to do the same.

Margaret responded to the checklist as follows:

- □ Being a parent is not easy.

  Loving your child is the easiest thing.

  Knowing what is the right thing to do is the most difficult thing.

  There are so many different things that crop up.

  It would be easier if I had more experience.

  Keeping her safe all the time... I haven't done that, have I?

  Sometimes it's difficult making the right decision.

- □ I love being a parent. Charlotte makes me feel alive.

  The best thing is seeing her grow...seeing her change. I remember her first word...her first step.

  The worst thing is when she is hurt or upset and I don't know what to do to make her feel better.

- □ I don't feel particularly confident with any age of child.

  I am looking forward to Charlotte as she grows up. I would not say that I am not looking forward to a particular age...that does not mean to say that I think I will not have any problems.

  I am probably most worried about how difficult it will be when she is a teenager.

- □ Love, my unconditional love...that's the most important thing I can give her.

  I comfort her when she cries.

  Sometimes I know she just cries for attention or wants something...but I have to cuddle her when she cries.

  Charlotte comes to me for attention...praise...when she has hurt herself...when she wants something.

  She comes to me all the time for all sorts of things.

I am her mother, she comes to me for everything.

❑ I have made lots of mistakes.

The biggest mistake is that I believed John when he said she kept falling. I believed him when he said he only tapped her. I did not know he was hitting her.

Why didn't she come to me and tell me?

The biggest mistake is not preventing Charlotte from being hurt. I should have protected her, she is my child…she is my responsibility.

❑ Yes…being hurt, no child should be hurt.

❑ School is important… I wasted my school… I should have said I was being bullied.

I will encourage Charlotte to go to school. I will read to her… I already do sometimes.

- Analyse the collective strengths and weaknesses of the perceptions of Margaret and John.

- Does any of the information give you child protection concerns?

- Which of the responses, if any, would you have explored further?

- Are there any additional questions you would have asked?

EXERCISE 23 – CASE STUDY FOR THE STRESS CHECKLIST

1.   Complete the questionnaire on stress based upon your own experiences. When you have done this, look at your responses. Recognise that we all suffer from stress to some extent. The stress checklist is designed to look at how stress affects the person generally, and to look at any specific areas of stress which might impact upon parenting abilities.

2.   Exercise on checklist answers.

❑ Yes I suffer from stress…doesn't everybody?

❑ People asking me personal questions makes me stressed.
Bills.

When things I have not expected crop up.

Problems...problems I don't have the answers for.

☐ Social workers stress me.

People who hassle me.

☐ My wife sometimes stresses me.

The kids sometimes.

People who hassle me.

People who don't listen...they make me angry, that makes me stressed.

☐ The children, they wind me up sometimes...that causes stress.

When they don't do as they are told...that stresses me when I feel really tired.

Worrying about them when they are out stresses me sometimes.

When I don't know where they are.

☐ When I am stressed I have an upset stomach.

Sometimes I get a headache.

Sometimes I feel really ill... Once I went to bed on Friday and stayed in bed all weekend. That was stress.

☐ It depends ... Sometimes I feel stressed every day...sometimes only once per week.

Sometimes I can go for weeks without stresses.

I don't feel stressed all the time...not all day every day.

☐ When I feel stressed I sometimes have a drink.

Sometimes I go for a walk.

Sometimes I like to be alone.

I am more inclined to lose my temper when I get stressed.

Sometimes I can be moody when I am stressed.

☐ No, I have never been to the doctor... Maybe I should have in the past.

☐ She is brilliant, she tries to take the pressure off me.

We talk... Sometimes she gives me a hug.

❑ Most of the time it works… Sometimes the only thing that works is when the problem has gone.

❑ My partner.

Having the time and space to sit down and sort things out.

Making the right decisions… It gives me a lift.

- Evaluate the positive and negative aspects of the comments made.
- How do you feel the person's responses have an impact on their parenting ability?
- Would you have wanted clarification of any of the responses?
- Are there any further questions on stress you would have asked?

EXERCISE 24 – CASE STUDY FOR PARENTAL STRESS

Cheryl is 19 years of age, she has three children, twins aged 2 and a baby of six months. Her partner, Jonathan, is currently serving a prison sentence for burglary. Cheryl has no relatives living nearby and has no friends in the neighbourhood.

Her responses to the checklist questions were:

❑ Yes, being a parent is stressful.

❑ They are active but no more than most children.

I do get really tired because they are a handful.

They are always on the go.

❑ They don't do things on purpose to wind me up but some of the things they do make me stressed.

They have no sense of danger and I worry about what they are doing.

❑ They are not more difficult than most children.

The baby cries a lot and I don't seem to be able to pacify her… I spend hours at night pacing the floor with her.

❑ They can go on and on until they get what they want… Don't all children. Sometimes I think they take it in turns just to wear me down.

❑ Yes, they do things to please me.

The twins know how to make me laugh.

☐ They love to play with me... I love playing with them.

Sometimes I feel too exhausted to play.

☐ I don't think they are miserable and unhappy.

Sometimes I think the twins are sad, I think they miss their father.

☐ Being a parent isn't harder than I thought.

Being a parent with no partner and three small children...that's about as hard as it gets.

☐ All children lose their temper...usually over silly things...but they don't think they are silly. My children are no different to most.

☐ Yes, they are always quick to pick things up.

I think they are very bright, even the baby.

☐ Making sure I am being fair to them is the most stressful thing about being a parent.

☐ My children are the same as others... I don't think they make more demands of me than other children.

If I think about it they are probably less demanding than most kids.

☐ They usually do as they are told.

The twins can be very disobedient sometimes... I know it is just them being kids but it does wind me up.

The twins go to a play group... They behave just the same.

It gives me a bit of a break, I get some peace and quiet.

☐ The baby can be a bit grumpy in the morning but the twins are okay. They wake up early though...and they can be noisy.

☐ They are too young to know what money is.

☐ Their behaviour doesn't make me angry...they are only kids.

I get so tired sometimes I lose my temper with them.

When the baby is crying, that makes me angry sometimes... Sometimes I get stressed.

❑ I have always felt close to my children. I am their mother... They are my kids.

❑ Yes. I don't have enough time to do all the things I want to do.

I never seem to have enough time to play with them.

❑ If Jonathan was around more...then he could share the responsibilities with me.

If I had more time.

If I had more money.

- Identify the areas of stress/difficulty for Cheryl.

- Does she find the general role of parenting stressful/difficult?

- Does she find any specific aspects of parenting the children stressful/difficult?

- Are there any additional questions you would have asked?

- Are there any answers you would have investigated further?

EXERCISE 25 – CASES STUDY FOR PARENTING KNOWLEDGE AND STYLE

Dean is 30 years of age. He left home when he was 16 and has lived by himself since that time. He has had two serious relationships but has always maintained his independence.

Following a brief relationship, his son Duane was born six months previously. Dean has no previous child care experience but wants to look after his son.

His responses to the checklist were:

❑ Babies cry because they want to be fed...they are hot...cold...they need their nappies changing. They may by teething, uncomfortable or ill.

❑ I think I would know the different types of crying by the tone of their voice.

I would like to think I would know.

I would sort Duane out, make him comfortable, stop him from crying.

❑ I don't know what physical needs Duane would have as he was growing up.

I would need to look after him.

Provide food, shelter, clothing.

- □ I don't know what emotional needs Duane would have. I have never looked after a child before.

- □ He would need to go to school for his education.

  Children learn by following others...going to school.

  There are education films...teachers.

  Parents can teach their children, and grandparents can too.

- □ Dangerous things are naughty.

  When children are cheeky...destructive.

  If they have tantrums.

  If they are disobeying, not doing as they are told.

- □ I would give Duane a small smack on the bum...little slaps...nothing to hurt...to let him know that I am there.

  I would ground him...stop his pocket money.

  I would stop the things that he likes doing.

  I would send him early to bed.

- □ I wouldn't like to think I would ever smack my child hard. I was hit and I did not like it.

  Little slaps are okay if he was being really naughty.

- □ I think that children like to be cuddled.

  I would cuddle him as much as he needed.

- □ Children should know that parents are in charge.

  Parents also need to take advice from their kids...it works both ways.

- □ Duane would know I was in charge.

  The way I brought him up he would know I was in charge.

  Saying no.

- □ Yes, parents should encourage imaginary play.

Yes, I would join in if Duane wanted me to.

I don't know what age he would be when he would want to stop having imaginary play. I have never looked after a child before.

Most grown ups have not grown out of things.

Maybe by the time he was eight.

Parents should play with children every day of their life.

All the while.

☐ I haven't got a clue how long a child of twelve months would concentrate on one thing.

I have never looked after a child before.

☐ It depends where the shop was and how busy the road was.

It depends where I lived and how safe it was.

Maybe when he has left school he could have a serious girlfriend.

I would be over-protective.

I would let Duane have a serious girlfriend after he had left school.

☐ He could be allowed to stay up until 10 o'clock when he was 14 or 15.

I would let him be allowed in the house alone when he was 14 or 15.

Kitchens are dangerous...there are lots of hazards.

He would be allowed in the kitchen unsupervised when he was about 15 or 16.

☐ Age would not come into it...if he was old enough to understand things like having a new partner...or moving house. There would be discussion.

☐ Age doesn't matter. Children should know the value of money...pocket money is important in that.

Even if I wasn't giving him money to spend, I would be putting it in a jar for him so that he would learn the value of saving...and the value of money.

☐ I would teach Duane about contraception, masturbation and safe sex when he was old enough to understand.

It's important that he doesn't get himself into trouble because I haven't told him enough.

I think they probably learn about these things at school as well.

Pornographic films should be banned.

Most adults I know have seen them but that doesn't make it right.

- Evaluate Dean's parenting style.
- What parenting knowledge would you say Dean has?
- Are there any further questions you would have asked?
- Would you have explored any of Dean's answers further?

EXERCISE 26 – CASE STUDY ON LIVING ARRANGEMENTS

Identify the arrangements which would be necessary for the good enough, safe enough care of a child.

What issues are likely to prevent a child being properly protected in the home environment?

EXERCISE 27 – CASE STUDY ON FINANCES

What financial priorities should a parent have in order to look after a child in ways which safeguard and promote their welfare?

EXERCISE 28 – CASE STUDY FOR CHILD PROTECTION CONCERNS

Sarah is 27 and has a son, Michael, aged 4. She has recently separated from Michael's father, Colin, following an incident in which Michael received 'bite mark' injuries which were subsequently proved to have been perpetrated by his father, Colin. There were similar, healing injuries of different ages.

Sarah responded to the checklist questions as follows.

- ❑ I believe that the social services department is concerned because Michael was bitten... They say it was Colin who did it.

I suppose they must be concerned because I was looking after Michael as well... I didn't realise what was happening.

They said I should have known what was happening... How could I have

    ❑ I suppose the concerns must be real...Michael has been injured.

      The bites weren't too bad.

      I don't think Colin would lose his temper again...if he came back here to live.

      They say it has happened more than once...I can't believe that.

      Michael can be difficult...he knows how to wind you up.

    ❑ Michael has been hurt by his father... I haven't been bitten before, I don't know how much it would hurt.

      I didn't do anything to him.

    ❑ Things are different now because I have left Colin.

      Sometimes I get really lonely without him.

    ❑ I understand from the social worker and from things which Michael has said that Colin lost his temper and bit Michael.

      Colin has never lost his temper before...not with Michael.

    ❑ I suppose Colin should not have done that... He could have hurt him really seriously.

    ❑ I haven't injured Michael but I should have protected him so that he was not hurt.

      I think I am more alert to that kind of danger now.

    ❑ I suppose I would be over-protective if I entered into a new relationship.

      I would be probably checking Michael all the time to see if he had any bumps or bruises.

      I am not sure whether it is over between me and Colin.

- Do you think that Sarah has a good understanding of the child protection concerns?

- What do you consider the child protection concerns to be?

- Were there any answers you would have explored further?

- Are there any additional questions you would have asked?

REFERENCES

Cleveland Report (1988) *Report of the Enquiry into Child Abuse in Cleveland 1987.* London: HMSO.

Clyde, Lord (1992) *Report of the Enquiry into the Removal of Children from Orkney in February 1991.* London: HMSO.

Department of Health (1988) *Protecting Children. A Guide for Social Workers Undertaking a Comprehensive Assessment.* London: HMSO.

Department of Health (1991) *Working together under the Children Act 1989.* London: HMSO.

Department of Health (1992) *Memorandum of Good Practice (on video-recorded interviews with child witnesses for criminal proceedings).* London: HMSO.

Department of Health (1995) *Child Protection: Messages from Research.* London: HMSO.

Department of Health (1998) *The Government's Response to the Children's Safeguards Review* (Cm 4105). London: The Stationery Office.

Department of Health (1999) *Working Together to Safeguard Children.* London: The Stationery Office.

Department of Health (2000) *Framework for the Assessment of Children in Need and their Families.* London: The Stationery Office.

Foster Placement (Children) Regulations (1991). SI 1991 no910

London Borough of Brent (1985) *A Child in Trust. The Report of the Panel of Enquiry into the Circumstances Surrounding the Death of Jasmine Beckford.* London: Borough of Brent.

London Borough of Greenwich (1987) *A Child in Mind: Protection of Children in a Responsible Society. The Report of the Commission of Enquiry into the Circumstances Surrounding the Death of Kimberley Carlile.* London: Borough of Greenwich.

London Borough of Lambeth (1987) *Whose Child? The Report of the Public Enquiry into the Death of Tyra Henry.* London: Borough of Lambeth.

Home Office, Department of Health, Department of Education and Science, Welsh Office (1989) *Working Together under The Children Act.* London: HMSO.

Morrison T. (1991) 'Change, control and the legal framework.' In Adcock M., White R. and Hollows A. (eds.) *Significant Harm.* London: Significant Publications.

Placement for Children with Parents etc. Regulations (1991). SI 1991 no893

Prochaska, J. and Diclemente, C. (1991) in Adcock, M., White, R. and Hollows, A. (eds.) *Significant Harm*. London: Significant Publications.

Rochdale, BC versus A and others (1991) 2 FLR (Family Law Report) 192.

Treacher, A., and Carpenter, J. (1989) *Problems and Solutions in Family and Marital Therapy*. London: Faber and Faber.

Treaty Series No. 44 of 1992 (Cm 1976), Adopted by the UN General Assembly on 20 November 1989. Ratified so far by 154 countries.

STATUTES

Adoption Act 1976 London: HMSO.

Child Care Act 1980. London: HMSO.

Children Act 1989. London: HMSO.

Children and Young Persons Act 1933. London: HMSO.

Children and Young Persons Act 1969. London: HMSO.

Human Rights Act 1998. London: HMSO.